Critique of
Instrumental
Reason

Lectures
and Essays
since the end
of
World War II

Critique of Instrumental Reason

by
MAX HORKHEIMER

Translated by Matthew J. O'Connell and others

A CONTINUUM BOOK

The Seabury Press / New York

The Seabury Press
815 Second Avenue
New York, N. Y. 10017

English translation copyright © 1974 by The Seabury Press

Designed by s. s. DRATE

Printed in the United States of America

Original edition: *Zur Kritik der instrumentellen Vernuft.*
© S. Fischer Verlag GmbH, Frankfurt am Main, 1967

Acknowledgments:

The essay *Theism and Atheism* was first translated from the German and published in *Diogenes,* Winter 1964, No. 48, an international quarterly published under the auspices of Unesco, Paris. Reprinted with permission. The essay *Schopenhauer Today* appeared first in translation in *The Critical Spirit: Essays in Honor of Herbert Marcuse,* ed. Wolff and Moore. Copyright © 1967 by Beacon Press.

Library of Congress Cataloging in Publication Data

Horkheimer, Max, 1895-1973.
  Critique of instrumental reason.

  (A Continuum book)
  Translation of Zur Kritik der instrumentellen Vernunft.
  1. Reason. 2. Civilization. I. Title.
B3279.H8473E3513   193   74-8450
ISBN 0-8164-9221-2

Contents

Foreword

"Reason" for a long period meant the activity of understanding and assimilating the eternal ideas which were to function as goals for men. Today, on the contrary, it is not only the business but the essential work of reason to find means for the goals one adopts at any given time. And it is considered superstitious to think that goals once achieved are not in turn to become means to some new goal. For centuries obedience to God was the means of winning his favor, but also the way to rationalize every kind of subjugation, crusades of conquest, and terrorism. Ever since Hobbes, however, men shaped by the Enlightenment, be they theists or atheists, have considered the commandments to be socially useful moral principles that will promote a life as free as possible from friction, peaceful relations between equals, and respect for the status quo. When stripped of its theological garb, "Be reasonable" means: "Observe the rules, without which neither the individual nor society as a whole can survive; do not think only of the present moment." Reason is considered to come into its own when it rejects any status as an absolute ("reason" in the intensified sense of the word) and accepts itself simply as a tool. It is true, of course, that there have in modern times been serious attempts to give a theoretical grounding for the claim that reason grasps absolute truth. A great part of modern philosophy since Descartes has striven to effect a compromise between theology and science, the agent in the transaction being "the faculty of intellectual ideas (the reason)." [1] In Kant's posthumously published papers we read: "What is divine about our soul is its capacity for ideas." [2] Nietzsche attacked this kind of belief in the autonomy of reason as a symptom of backwardness: "The German sense of values" finds "Locke and Hume . . . too luminous, too clear." [3] Kant he considered to be "retarded." [4] "Reason is merely an instrument, and Descartes is superficial." [5] As it has in other areas of a culture touched by decadence, the twentieth century has here seen history repeating itself. In 1900, the year of Nietzsche's death, Husserl published his *Logische Untersuchungen,* which was a new effort to give a strictly scientific basis for the claim that we perceive spiritual reality and have an intuition of essences. Husserl himself was thinking primarily of logical categories, but Max Scheler and others extended the doctrine to moral structures as well. The enterprise was marked from the beginning by an effort to turn the clock back. For it is an inner necessity that has led to the self-surrender by reason of its status as a spiritual substance. The function of theory today is to reflect upon and give expression to the whole process which we have here briefly indicated: the socially conditioned tendency toward neo-Positivism or the instrumentalization of thought, as well as the vain efforts to rescue thought from this fate.

In response to requests that a complete collection of my writings might be published, I decided for the moment only on a selection of pieces that had appeared

since the mid-forties. They were written in the time left
free from my practical activities: the organization of
Studies of Prejudice, academic administration, the revita-
lizing of the Institute for Social Research, and efforts at
educational reform. I am well aware that the wishes expressed to me related to the period in which the critical
theory took shape, especially in the essays I wrote for the
Zeitschrift für Sozialforschung, of which I was editor, as
well as in my unpublished studies and, not least, in
Dialektik der Aufklärung which I wrote with my friend,
Theodor Adorno, and which has long been out of print.[6]
At the end of the Nazi period (I though at the time)
a new day, the beginning of an authentically human history, would dawn in the developed countries as the result
of reforms or revolution. Along with the other founders of
Scientific Socialism, I thought that the cultural gains of
the bourgeois era—the free development of human
powers, a spiritual productivity—but stripped now of all
elements of force and exploitation, would surely become
widespread throughout the world.

My experiences since that time have not failed to
affect my thinking. The "communist" states, which make
use of the same Marxist categories to which my own
efforts in the realm of theory owe so much, are certainly
no closer to the dawn of that day than are the countries
in which, for the moment at least, the freedom of the
individual has not yet been snuffed out. Given this situation, I decided that, along with some other studies, my
various reflections on reason should be the first essays to
appear in a collection. These reflections, which underlie
my earlier studies as well, support, I hope, the contention
that the rule of freedom, once brought to pass, necessarily turns into its opposite: the automatizing of society

and human behavior. The pieces brought together here are efforts at reflection under the awareness of that contradiction, and without losing sight of either side of it.

Selection and revision are the work of Dr. Alfred Schmidt. Without his understanding and dedication this volume could not have appeared.

May, 1967   MAX HORKHEIMER

Critique of
Instrumental
Reason

THE CONCEPT OF MAN
(1957)

When contemporary philosophers speak of man, they seldom fail to note that the fundamental philosophical problem, the problem of being as such, is inseparable from the problem of man. At least in Europe in recent times, philosophy, including existentialism (the philosophy of concrete existence) is characterized by the fact that in it the doctrine of being as such arises, if not objectively, then at any rate in the process of reflection, only after the effort to win insight into man.

Such a state of affairs would seem to be due to the very nature of the question, if nothing else. For one thing, man the knower is himself part of the totality, of the world and all it contains; he is therefore able to perceive within himself, and perhaps even more clearly there than elsewhere, the being with which he must come to grips philosophically. In addition, an understanding of the very question of being, and consequently of the conditions which any response must satisfy and to which indeed any response is antecedently subject, require man's entering into himself and especially into his own thinking and philosophizing. In this respect, the most recent ontological philosophy is following in the footsteps of that older critical philosophy which it rejects. Classical German idealism began with an analysis of thought, with a rigorous exposition of the requirements which metaphysical answers must meet, with the critique of reason. The now dominant ontological trend likewise turned its attention first of all to the meaning of philosophical questions and then proceeded to man and finally to that being which supposedly embraces every individual reality and the questioner himself. Ontology is thus related to German idealism in many respects, and perhaps it is again discovering behind hidden being, as idealism did behind the unknowable thing-in-itself, the subject and spirit and activity. Yet the tone of both question and answer is different today, and it is worth our while to dwell briefly on it.

Kant reduced the concern with man to three questions: "What can I know? What ought I to do? What may I hope?"[1] The third question, which is "at once practical and theoretical,"[2] includes the other two. Examination of this third question leads to the idea of the highest good and absolute justice. The moral conscience, upon the truth of which depends the difference between good and evil, rebels against the thought that the present state of reality is final and that undeserved misfortune and wrongdoing, open or hidden, and not the self-sacrificing deeds of men, are to have the last word. Kant, therefore, no less than Voltaire or Lessing, postulates eternity. The postulate of a transcendental world is identical, in his philosophy, with the judgment on the immanent world. What mediates between the two, however, is not faith alone nor interiority but human life. Reality indeed does not seem able to promise fulfillment of man's claims on it, but this does not mean that the idea of the world "in so far as it may be in accordance with all the ethical laws"—in other words, the idea of a just order of things—"may [not] have, and ought [not] to have, an influence on the world of sense, so as to bring it as far as possible into conformity with itself." [3] Such is the consequence of man's autonomy. Kant's assurance that the realization of right order and the removal of contradictions belong to the infinite, intelligible world, is intended to help bring about change in the finite world. Hope that urges men on and guides their action is a constitutive element in the Kantian system and plays a role in even the subtlest transcendental analyses, as it is does not in mere epistemology.

In the critical view of man, therefore, an essential role belongs to the idea of a moral order and the conception of a world in which human merit and happiness are not simply juxtaposed but necessarily connected and in which injustice has disappeared. Kant, according to his own testimony, was "set straight" by Rousseau and would regard himself as "more useless than a common laborer" if his meditations could not contribute to "re-establishing the rights of mankind." [4] In this he is typical of the eighteenth century. The embarrassment which the militant Enlightenment causes contemporary philosophy, the neglect of its constitutive elements even in interpreting Kant, the superficiality which has been achieved through depth (as one Hegelian puts it) in the last few decades, the passage from critique to the positivistic stance and to concreteness—all this is proof not of an advance but only of resignation.

In the historical period after Kant the material conditions needed for a rational administration of the world improved to a degree undreamt of. Yet those who inherited these improved conditions are far from drawing the Kantian conclusion. Instead they have begun to speak of man in a different fashion. In the century of Enlightenment free thought was the force that knocked the solid supports of stupidity from under institutions which bad conscience had driven to adopt terroristic methods; it was the force that gave the bourgeoisie its self-awareness. In our own time, on the contrary, the feeling is abroad that free thought is helpless. Mastery of nature has not brought man to self-realization; on the contrary, the status quo continues to exert its objective compulsion. The factors in the contemporary situation—population growth, a technology that is becoming fully automated, the centralization of economic and therefore political power, the increased rationality of the individual as a result of his work in industry—are inflicting upon life a degree of organization and manipulation that leaves the individual only enough spontaneity to launch himself onto the path prescribed for him.

Where the word "man," therefore, is still used in a more pregnant sense, it does not imply the rights of mankind. It does not stand for a theory of reason such as once was based on the unshakable belief that a just world could still be brought into existence. The word "man" no longer expresses the power of the subject who can resist the status quo, however heavily it may weigh upon him. Quite differently than in the context of critical philosophy, to speak of man today is to engage in the endless question of the ground of man and, since in ontological philosophy ground supplies direction, in the endless quest for an image of man that will provide orientation and guidance. Speakers tirelessly challenge men and assure philosophers, sociologists, economists, and not least, the representatives of the economy and government, that "everything depends on the individual." To the extent that the speakers are not simply, though quite legitimately, looking for qualified young people who are masters of their jobs (we are told in a periodical that the demand for "personality" is quite universally voiced today [5]), what they have in mind, especially in Europe, is the strong individual who stands out against the system. Such an individual is to be a symbol of the fact that there can be such individuals. We must note, however, that when man is regarded as a spiritual being and not as a biological species, he is always a definite individual, not the dimensionless abstraction, distilled from the individuals of every social stratum, class, country, and age, such as those who ride in the antitheoretical train declare to be the concrete reality. Now, do those who exhort us really think that an individual can escape the objective forces which coerce and put their mark on him from his earliest years? Do they think that any individual who is still capable of resistance would allow himself to be guided, even in his sleep, by the deceitful image of the supposedly authentic and real, and not rather by his own insight into relations as they really are, by his awareness of the unity of all living things, and by the desire that everything should turn out right?

The acknowledgment of abstract man as though he were the one to avert the evil that lurks behind all our economic miracles, sounds like both a referral and an appeasement. *Physical* suffering under injustice and under the complication of an existence which despite the rise in living standards and expectations is becoming ever more difficult and insecure, is fobbed off by referring it to the insight that the important thing is personality. *Psychic* suffering is assuaged by conjuring up figures, past and present, who are proof that one can still be a man and not part of the masses to which no one wants to belong. The call for the real, authentic man is a call for models and examples and, all too easily, for leaders and fathers. Conceptual thought that is alienated from theory has become so malleable that it is mesmerized by any star from the worlds of power and film if he can but slip inside its defenses with the help of publicity. The so-called "authentic" man, no less than the being that has been materialized into a subject of research for run-of-the-mill philosophers, is but an empty well from which those who cannot achieve their own private life, their own decisions and inner power, fill up their dreams. In a typical book in praise of being and of the mind that inquires into it we read: "The person who finds himself engaged in this world of functions, whether it be a question of organic, psychological, professional, or social functions in the broadest sense, experiences deep within himself the need that there be *being*." [6] The vague profundity of the philosopher and, to no lesser degree, the popular idea that man will rescue us turn attention away from the real totality with its injustice and from the diversified interaction, overt and covert, between society and the individuals who are determined by society and determine it in turn, and direct that attention to the promising symbol of authentic reality. The symbol is then all too easily given its specific meaning by the great historical periods; theology is not indeterminate enough for the purpose. The idea of God and man which hides behind the doctrine of being and concrete existence carries with it a traditional sense. Even the relation of infinite and finite, as conceived by the idealists, still retains a utopistic element which has disappeared from the relation between being and concrete existence.

Theoretical reflection can assist in achieving liberation from this anthropological or existential deception. What is needed is converse with the great philosophers; I am thinking, for example, of Hegel's *Phenomenology of Mind* and his *Logic*. He made us aware of the superstition of the isolated, independent being and the absolutization of immediate experiences as well as of being and all that claims to be being. What is needed, further, is a knowledge of the theological tradition, for our grasp of the inextricable meshing of human freedom and its conditionings, as well as the Kantian hope, have their historical roots in that tradition. What is needed, no less importantly, is the contradiction-filled whole which is body and spirit, and the interconnection between society and individual of which that whole is a part. The belief which declares the abstract concepts of being and man to be concrete reality depends for its existence on decadence in education. Productive negation, on the contrary, depends at every point on solid education. It is impossible to oppose falsity without falling prey to it, unless the knowledge won by past and present generations is kept alive.

In the following remarks I shall be concerned simply to clarify, in contrast to the talk about man which I mentioned above, what is meant by the influence of society and individual on each other, an interaction in which society with its institutions today exercises by far the greater pressure. The knowledge that man's existence is mediated by society and history does not justify resignation, for the reverse is also true: that history is just as much related to man. But if that dependence on society is not fully perceived, it perpetuates itself. Fatalism, or despair about man's power to determine his own destiny and to intervene in the course of events, is far more likely to spring from the dark overtones of talk about being and from exaggerated, rootless ideas about a supposed authenticity, than it is from the critical attempt to understand the influential forces that shape and move men for good or for ill.

The action of society on the individual begins at his birth, if not sooner. We need not ask here what significance the mother's health and the nourishment and care given the child have for his future both physically and psychically. In great measure these factors depend on the wealth of the country, the present state of science, and the social status of the parents. After the initial months, mother love—the thing everyone talks about but rarely describes in any precise fashion—becomes decisive. Maternal love does not consist simply in feeling or even in attitude; it must also express itself properly. The wellbeing of the little child and the trust he has in people and objects around him depend very largely on the peaceful but dynamic friendliness, warmth, and smile of the mother or her substitute. Coldness and indifference, abrupt gestures, restlessness and displeasure in the one who attends the child can introduce a permanent distortion into his relationship to objects, men, and the world, and produce a cold character that is lacking in spontaneous impulses. This was recognized, of course, as far back as Rousseau's *Emile* and John Locke, and even earlier. Only today, however, are people beginning to grasp the factors involved in the connection of which we are speaking. It does not take a sociologist to recognize that a mother who is pressed by other cares and occupations has a different effect than the one she wants.

In the first year of life, before the human being is able to reflect and to distinguish himself properly from his surroundings, he is already in good measure being determined by society, right down to those aspects of his being which will develop only much later. For, among the capabilities which every man possesses as a biological being is the ability to assimilate and imitate. His behavior and gestures, his tone of voice, his very walk are all an echo in the child of the ways of some loved and admired adult. Psychic reactions are acquired, in the form if not their content; moreover, if a rigid separation of form and content leads to error in the analysis of a work of art, how much more in the interpretation of human feelings! Sadness and happiness, attention sought and given, shyness and devotion come into existence with the repetition of behavior and gestures, for, as Goethe says, "the outward is the inward." What we thoughtlessly ascribe to psychic heritage originates to a decisive degree in the impressions and reactions of earliest childhood, and is confirmed and modified by the circumstances and events of later years. Whether a man is bent on promoting his ego or is capable of vital interest in objective situations and of dedication to men and things; whether his thinking and even his sensibility are superficial or deep—all this is not simply a matter of natural fact but is the outcome of a history. The social position of his parents and their relationship to each other play a role in the process, as do the internal and external structure of the family and, indirectly, the ethos of the whole age. The character of an individual is no less determined by the time, place, and circumstances of his rearing than by the language he speaks, which shapes his very being and influences his thinking, and by his political situation of freedom or slavery and his religion.

Classical German philosophy has quite clearly formulated the non-independence of the individual being: "To have an individual, there is need of other realities which likewise appear to have an independent existence of their own; only in all of these taken together, with their interrelationships, is the concept fully realized. The individual as such does not correspond to its concept." [7] In other words, the individual is *real* only as part of the whole to which he belongs. His essential determinations, his character and inclination, his avocation and view of the world all have their origin in society and in his destiny within society. To what extent the society of any given moment itself corresponds to its own concept and thus to reason, is admittedly not settled.

The totality with which we are dealing here is not static but subject to internal movement. As the transition occurred from the bourgeois order of the beginning of the century (an order that was still in a semi-liberal stage) to the phase in which industrial power came to control everything, the change in man that was involved became fully clear. The child now grows up in a different kind of family; he becomes a different kind of individual than he would have been in conditions where a stratum of numerous independent entrepreneurs acting on their own initiative was a determining factor. The child now acquires a different kind of self-awareness. The fact that in the still intact bourgeois family the father was both loved and feared was not significant solely for the latter in his role as procreator or even as provider. Rather, he in his turn depended on his son for the continuation of his own active role in society. In influential circles the young man was the heir and destined to take over from his father the business or factory which the latter in turn had received from his father. At the very least the young man must follow a profession that accorded with his social position, and thus bring honor to his name. The concern with his son, which admittedly could turn a father into a tyrant, was the basis and consequence of the father's effective functioning as a member of the bourgeosie.

At the present time education is tending to replace the narrow purpose of continuing the parents' life through the children, with the broader one of producing successful individuals who can stand up for themselves in the contemporary battle of life. The father no longer finds support for himself in a special future for his children; this becomes clear when we observe the liquidation of the remnants of the bourgeois class and the decreasing significance of individualist entrepreneurship. The characteristic social type today is the employee. His relationship to his children is rather that of an older and more experienced comrade to a younger person; in the advanced countries and advanced social strata strictness is being replaced by a toleration and readiness to help that are associated with new ideas in education. The changes in society mean that even the mother is pushed more and more into work outside the home; this of course makes new claims on her psychic capacities and interests. In the nineteenth century the upper-class family guaranteed a lengthy and protected childhood and, as a late reflection of feudal hierarchy, gave rise, in favorable circumstances, to a sense of security, trust, and direction or, in unfavorable circumstances, to parental tyranny and filial resentment. But the family of today has surrendered many of its remaining functions to other institutions or to society at large.

Today's young man leaves the family a less encumbered person, but he pays for this with the loss of the interiority that had formerly been developed during the interaction which went on throughout a long childhood. In that earlier day the father was in large measure a free man. The outcome of his action in society did not, of course, depend on him alone. At least, however, no other will—neither of leader nor of group—made his decisions for him. As long as he stayed within the law, he was subject to no one and responsible only to his own conscience. He was his own master and for that very reason his rule did not have to take the form of tyranny. In favorable conditions he became for his child an example of autonomy, resoluteness, self-command, and breadth of mind. For his own sake he required of his child truthfulness and diligence, reliability and intellectual alertness, love of freedom and discretion, until these attitudes, having been internally assimilated by the child, became the normative voice of the latter's own conscience and eventually, in the conflicts of puberty, set him at odds with his father. Today the child is much more directly thrown upon society, childhood is shortened, and the result is a human being cast in a different mold. As interiority has withered away, the joy of making personal decisions, of cultural development, and of the free exercise of imagination has gone with it. Other inclinations and other goals mark the man of today: technological expertise, presence of mind, pleasure in the mastery of machinery, the need to be part of and to agree with the majority or some group which is chosen as a model and whose regulations replace individual judgment. Advice, prescriptions, and patterns for guidance replace moral substance.

The change in individuals is but the reverse side of social change. Not only the basis which once gave unity to the bourgeois family, but the very meaning of the qualities such a family produced have become outdated. The specific relationship of the large-scale merchant to his "business friends" at home or abroad, which in Wilhelm Meister's time involved a significant measure of cultivated exchange, is no less a thing of the past than the old-time relationship of client to lawyer or doctor. In similar fashion the civilian used to expect the academic man to be, not a professional, but a more educated counselor, one superior to himself in humanistic ways. The division of labor has long since, however, become more complex, life has become more rigidly organized, and in our part of the world, the cultural differences between nations and classes have been too leveled down for there to be need of a wide-ranging educational formation in order to bridge them. Public relationships, like private, have become the domain of the expert; in the eighteenth century men had little treatises on how to deal with people, in the twentieth whole professions occupy themselves with this matter. Personal views and convictions, and a general yet differentiated education are losing their usefulness. And once the dynamic urge is gone which a practical interest in the preservation of elements of culture gave, the corresponding dimension of human character disappears as well. For this reason the struggle against the reduction of the university to a professional school is doomed to failure. The education that once was supported by a felt social need is degenerating into a high-class psychic preparation, a kind of intellectual prophylaxis effected by means of recordings and paperbacks for mass consumption. Education, in abbreviated or unabbreviated form, edited, filmed, and synchronized for sound, is being given to a far greater majority, but in the process it suffers a radical change of function, somewhat as the city woman's robe, once transplanted into the villages by lady's maids and servants, became the peasant woman's costume. Classical and European culture as inwardly assimilated by the individual, personal cultivation in the specific sense given the term by Humanism and German Idealism, is being replaced by modes of sensibility and behavior which are proper to a technicized society.

The realization that young men and women today are, at bottom, different even from what they were at the beginning of this century seems to contradict the notion that the decisive elements in man are unchangeable; in other words, that through all change in appearance the essence abides. In fact, however, the old principle that man is a rational animal, "a compound of soul and body," [8] and with it the whole of traditional anthropology have not lost their validity. But their meaning differs depending on whether the distinction between essential attributes and the phenomenal qualities of the individual is made according to a discursive or a dialectical logic. In trying to rescue the permanence of concepts you may, of course, turn every essential trait and intellectual manifestation into a genus with such wide meshes that it retains its validity against all the phenomena (be they individual beings or qualities of the latter) which fall under it. You can interpolate as mediating links new species and, like subtle Scotus, all kinds of "thisness," and thus erect a hierarchy that moves from ideal essences down to mutable realities. Every change in the social whole with which the meaning and content of human traits are bound up would then require new psychological or even anthropological subcategories and varieties, as in the specimen-drawer system used in the classificatory sciences of a bygone era. The only things that would remain unchanged through the ages are overpowering physical pain and all the extreme situations in which man is no longer master of himself and is thrust out of his societally-oriented spiritual existence back into nature.

In contrast to such a statistical conception, the man of a given social stratum and period, and each of his traits as well, can be viewed in such a way that the definition given of him and his traits remains in principle fully open to possible and indeed necessary changes in it. For however much history may depend on individuals who submit or rebel, on rulers and ruled, victors and victims, it remains true that man's makeup is itself a product of his history. In its inmost meaning it is relative to the social forms of the life and culture to which it belongs, even if it is by no means simply reducible to these. The social whole ceases to act as an external force marking the very being of the individuals who make it up, only to the extent that the rational spontaneity proper to society becomes the transparent principle of the individual's existence. Rousseau and Hegel saw in the objective Spirit and in society and state a second nature. If this second nature is to slough from itself the irrationality proper to the first, it is not enough for men to recognize themselves in it; the recognition must be legitimate. In other words, society becomes rational only to the extent that it fulfills the Kantian hope.

Until this happens, the attributes of man are subject to the power of a whole that is alien to him. This whole controls the change in love between man and woman no less than it controls the meaning of childhood. The fact that the girl in a bourgeois family was called upon to keep house for her future husband and to give him heirs determined the content and purpose of her education and moral training; it determined her self-awareness and expectations of happiness; it regulated her behavior. But even after the gradual extension of her rights in modern times the young woman did not become a genuinely free subject. Philosophy from the Greeks down to German Idealism has both expressed and justified this state of affairs by maintaining that woman is not a wholly mature and responsible being. Following Aristotle's lead, the great Scholastic theologians explained the very "procreation of a female" as due to unfavorable circumstances, whether "because of deficient active force or unreadiness of material" or as "the result of some quite extraneous circumstance." [9] Man was the complete being, woman a male manqué, a sort of inferior male. However perfect the community may be, the virtues of woman fit her simply to serve; they relate her to man through whom alone she may exercise any influence on public life.

The conflict that has marked our history since the Renaissance has thus determined the very nature of woman, who was still unable, in Kant's view, to choose her own husband and must not marry "against her parents' will." [10] Her nature, unlike that of man, was not shaped by activity in the labor market and adapted to circumstances outside the home. Yet her passive role, which nothing could justify, also enabled her to avoid reduction to object-status and thus to represent, amid an evil society, another possibility. In the passage from the old serfdom to the new she could be regarded as a representation of nature, which eluded utilitarian calculation. This element, regardless of whether woman was opposing society or submitting to it, determined her image for the bourgeois era. By renouncing any concern for her personal life and following her man in self-forgetfulness, the young girl was to reach her own self-fulfillment. The disobedience to family and society which a woman might unquestioningly accept for love's sake despite her having been educated and destined for service, her ability to love in contradiction to the world's norms, was not simply one factor but the dominant trait in the picture of the young girl and even of the mother; it marked her inner being no less than her outward behavior. No poetry gave fuller expression to this aspect of woman than did the German, in which the unconditionedness, the irreversibility, the imminence of death gave love its sweetness.

In view of the changes which have occured in the family in the age of full employment, however, Julia, Gretchen, and even Madame Bovary are now but curiosities. A woman's "false step" has lost its tragic character and no longer puts her into an irremediable state. This does not mean that a woman's professional prospects today are equal to man's; society is still a man's society. It does mean that though she has not won emancipation, woman in our manipulated society can make decisions like those of men. It is no longer the traits which once enabled her to avoid reduction to object-status, but those which today requires, that develop in the explicit forms modernity calls for. Woman must win mastery of life. Love, which no longer plays such a decisive role, is coming to resemble comradeship. Marriage no longer means such a radical change in her existence. The equation of woman and sex is disappearing; woman is becoming an economic subject in one or another sector of the division of labor, including the household sector. Thus not only the old social classes but even the pre- and post-marital states are becoming less differentiated. In marriage the relations between the partners must, above all, be rich in results, like those of teams in industry and sport. If a marriage proves burdensome it can be dissolved, and a person may perhaps be more successful with a new partner. Each partner is evaluated in terms of function, and this affects even the relations of the sexes before marriage, so that these relations become more uniform, more practical, less charged with momentous significance. Our mechanized world, which at present is assimilating man to itself, as well as the invasion of private existence by the machine and the acquisitive spirit, are stripping the romantic love tragedy of its historical relevance, although the tragedies themselves have not become rarer in this age of hasty decisions. The young woman and the young man, though oriented to each other by their sexual natures, stand against each other at the rational level, and their relationship is taking on a new quality, especially since young people now have a more important place in society.

As technology is being revolutionized and becoming widespread, an economic structure is developing which favors the young at the expense of older people. The old-style business firm needed the qualities which could only be developed in the course of a long life. From this fact came the high value placed on experience in the general consciousness. Modern mechanized complexes, on the contrary—be they the material ones in the factory workroom or the personal ones in the administrative offices—demand accuracy and energy rather than wisdom. When, in addition, total automation requires very highly developed abilities, the latter, found in relatively young men, represent an important investment for the company. Only with difficulty can the necessary training be acquired by older men. It is true, of course, that the commanders of the mighty corporations play a far more significant role in relation to mankind than did the managers of the old counting-houses. But, somewhat like military commanders, these men leave innumerable functions to the general staff which looks after details. In a factory, as formerly in war, even the most important decisions are a matter for the quick mind rather than for experience. In Korea the chances of an attack at this or that point were calculated by a computer into which all the available data concerning manpower, equipment, and terrain were fed (think of all Napoleon still had to depend on his own judgment for!). So too the heads of the mammoth corporations receive from computers, which are more reliable than men, an overview of their world-wide activities and a preview of the course of these activities and of the economy as a whole. Civil affairs and military, war and peace, are all interlocked.

The great old masters of economy and administration, especially in the political sphere, are only a seeming counterargument. For what is characteristic of the economy now is not that older men can no longer reach certain heights in society. It is rather that in growing measure the young *too* can do the job and, at many points, do it better, and that not a few positions which at one time had to be filled by older men are now being eliminated by technology. The effects of the changed economy are heightened by the changed role of the father in the modern family, of which we have already spoken. The same kind of development shows in the lowering of the age at which people marry. The economy today pronounces men independent at an earlier age, although not independent in the old bourgeois sense. In comparison with older men these young people are not mature but they are without illusion, perplexed, and clever. What is happening is a mirror image of the social revolution in eighth- and ninth-century Europe, which affected the deepest levels of man's nature. At that time the transition took place from the age of the young military leaders and conquerors to the age of settlement in which instead of courage and rashness caution and adherence to tradition became decisive qualities.[11] This whole process is now being reversed at a higher level. It is as impossible to halt it as it would have been to make greater age an advantage in the days of the pioneers when North America was being colonized. The only question is whether in the phase upon which mankind is now entering the cultural qualities of past ages will, while undergoing a change, be carried over as part of the coming civilization, or whether they will simply be eliminated and have to be rediscovered later on.

The fact that through its alliance with technology youth is regaining its ancient advantage over age signifies the removal of an historically conditioned but now untenable distinction rather than the emergence of a new cultural quality, such as happened when experience came to be prized. The clarity and penetration which are replacing experience show their presence more quickly than experience did and at an earlier age. The search for such qualities as used to require a lengthy and, as it were, organic maturation is becoming less important as rationalization increases. Those qualities are now being sacrificed to the very principle which originally led to their development, and they are now receiving the kind of reverential tribute we give to museum pieces. The chemistry which is now outmoding age even biologically is simply ratifying the thrust of the economy. The leveling down touches everything, even power and weakness.

Like the opposition between the ages of life, the opposition between city and countryside too is being reduced. It is well known that the takeover of the market by large-scale industry is moving forward in agriculture no less than in the manufacturing sector. In Europe, the continued juxtaposition of numerous individual cities (really an outdated phenomenon) is hindering this tendency, like a blockage in traffic. Yet even here the small farmer (the only farmer in the proper sense of the word) no less than the artisan is learning from personal experience that he has been born out of time. Government aid, the wealth of many farmers, and the great farm-complexes simply confirm that the day is now past when the city-dweller could think of the farmer's life, in contrast with his own, as the only proper way to live. The glorification of farm life as the perennially human situation cannot stand up to criticism any better than the contempt heaped on that same life in the days when Luther was summoning men to battle. The small farmer's wish is no longer simply for a tractor but for an automobile. He is urged to this not only by his personal economic situation but by the general style of life into which he is inexorably being drawn. The picture of the dead city and the living village that we find in Stefan George's poetry (*Der siebente Ring*) is no longer relevant (if indeed it ever was), simply because the two things being compared do not co-exist. The superiority of quiet valleys that have no landscapes to draw attention and no summer visitors to fill them is now appreciated only by connoisseurs; the very appearance of such places only rouses yearning for the city in the livelier village youth. On the other hand, when closeness to the city sets the tone of life and the quiet has vanished, when the filling stations point the way to go and come, then every shop is bent on rivaling its fellows in the city and every menu apes the city restaurant, unless a type of cooking proper to the place in generations past is now offered as a specialty in an effort to make the traveler stop. But in fact you get a more robust whole-meal break in your city delicatessen; and the wines, the recent vintages of which, like human beings, are winning out over the older ones, can more readily be found in the city than along the Rhine where the grapes are grown.

For their part the cities are now becoming indistinguishable from the villages. The transformation of village into suburb by incorporation is a Europe-wide expedient. The newer continental cities are, in the phrase of an expert observer, stretching out into the countryside like great beasts. Since the skyscrapers of the inner cities are occupied by offices and their appendages, people are moving their living quarters ever further out, and the noise follows them. Quiet becomes the privilege of the occasional especially elegant neighborhood. Since, moreover, the need for office space steadily increases as new businesses and factories arise, the character of various sections of the city is in constant flux. Old streets become thoroughfares crowded with the private automobiles which each owner must himself drive and park. On the now vanishing perimeters cities and countryside blend into each other, while the suburban market centers are coming to resemble modernized villages and vice versa. Civilization has always gone forth from the cities: the countryside accepted religion and the breakdown of religions, theaters and morals, from the cities; now it has unquestioningly adopted newspaper, cinema, radio, and television. And the city comes half-way to meet the countryside. The pastoral plays of the Rococo age have their prosaic counterpart in the exaggeratedly careless dress of city youth with their bright-colored shirts and blue jeans. The higher degree of cultivation among the peasants matches the cities' return to ruder ways.

Machinery requires, for its operation no less than its invention, the kind of mentality that concentrates on the present and can dispense with memory and straying imagination. To find one's way around the jungle of city life with its machinery leaves no time or inclination for anything else; the release of tension is therefore sought in traveling great distances, in free movement, and, for hygienic reasons, in rest. The taste which family and factory direct to the immediate object of the moment seeks to exercise itself, even in so-called leisure time, on the multiplicity and changing quality of some kind of object, on the ordering and mastery of material reality; thus the capacity for experience that transcends the immediate situation is being atrophied. The cities, as sociologists could learn from the literary men, have on the whole promoted tolerance and freedom. The fact that each individual must daily take into consideration countless others who he does not even know, the fact that he accustoms himself to meet them, to look at them without gazing into their inner selves, to attend to their interests even while he pursues his own—all this gave him at one time the restless nervous temperament which Georg Simmel has described in such masterly fashion. But that too is now disappearing. Given social mobility and the rapid change in social roles, each person must be prepared to have his fellow-worker at the factory later become his foreman, his supplier a competitor, his neighbor a political functionary if not his immediate neighborhood overseer. This develops in him the reserve and suspicion of strangers which used to be characteristic of village life. Conversation becomes superficial, convictions a burden. The various machines—record player, radio, television—which do away with speech even among friends have made their appearance just at the right moment. They provide models for behavior and give muteness the illusion that something is being said. Despite his ability to think quickly the city-dweller is losing the habit of self-expression. Since, however, speech cannot be replaced by signs without the inner reality which speech conveys also being impoverished, city life in its most recent phase is fostering a shriveling of the very spirit it once developed in opposition to the dull superstition of the countryside; this in turn brings a distortion of personality.

If the distinctions between professions, between village and city, working hours and leisure time, child and young person, feminine and masculine frames of mind are now being leveled, then men are becoming like one another without drawing any closer together. Thus it is not only the mechanization of life but even the earlier age at which people marry that is effecting not solidarity but

fragmentation among men. Among Kant's marginal nota-
tions we find the remark: "The man with a wife is complete; he separates himself from his parents and is now
simply in a state of nature." [12] Kant is thinking of Hobbes
and that rudeness which characterized man's state before civilization but which continues to exist even in
civilization. Marriage in bourgeois society limited the
man's unfocused interests in the sense that henceforth he
approached others in his life outside the home less with a
desire for community than as an economic agent in the
competitive struggle. In compensation, the domestic life
of the family was, for good or for ill, structured along
patriarchal lines and acknowledged the man's domination; relationships there did not depend on contribution
or accomplishment. Today, however, the principle of
equality is penetrating even into the family, and the contrast between private and social spheres is being blunted.
The emancipation of woman means that she must be the
equal of her husband: each partner in the marriage (the
very word "partner" is significant) is evaluated even
within the home according to the criteria that prevail in
society at large. Even marriage is an exchange between
equals, whether the measure be material or spiritual, and
each party must receive his due. Thus at the moment
when a culture based on equal exchange is threatened,
such exchange is becoming the complete norm for the
closest of human relationships; the personal sphere is being rationalized. How many circumstances are conspiring
to disaccustom the individual to friendship, despite all
the increased cultivation of acquaintances, all the proli-
feration of consultations, conferences, business trips, and
tourist journeys, and all the energy put into organizing
much-heralded "conversations" and "encounters"! Behind
the stereotyped smile and the diligent optimism the isola-

tion is growing more intense. We have already mentioned
how the young man, even of the upper classes, is forced
at a much earlier age to look after his own interests and
therefore is the captive of the goals he pursues. An at age
when the well-off used to be free of responsibility and
worry about career and, unburdened by secondary concerns, had time for study and travel, the young man of
today must keep a resolute eye on external goals. He is
marked by a peculiar prevailing seriousness which suggests not so much any insight into wretchedness and injustice as that the wings of imagination have been clipped
too soon. No one today learns to devote his leisure to anything but the much-praised "concrete reality," that is, to
accomplishments that are very much like work: doing
amateur repairs, driving an auto, sitting at machines; even
the idea of an old age free of toil no longer awakens any
great yearning.

The time society has gained through technology is
organized in advance for the individual. The shortening
of the workday is partially cancelled out in America by
the greater size of the overpopulated cities, in Germany
by the housing shortage. The work which the average
modern man must do at home has been increased not
only by changes within the family but also by shifts in the
price-structure. The little things made by hand are now
more expensive in comparison with large appliances and
mass-produced goods. Not only the worker and employee
but also the upper classes who are not at quite the highest
level have their time taken up by private and professional
duties, on the one hand, and by necessary rest, on the
other; thus they are losing the leisure which culture requires. As late as 1900 the employer could go to work in
a not very crowded railroad car and might walk home;
in the years before World War I he shifted to a chauffered

automobile. Today, maids and chauffeurs and all personal servants have become a luxury available only to a very few. Everyone is always busy. The time is gone when a sick person would listen for the hoof beat of the horse that pulled the doctor's cart through the still streets in the late evening. Today, like any tradesman, the doctor sits at the wheel of his own car and must be on the alert if he is to get through traffic safely. The number of his patients increases due to the competition which technology has intensified, and any thoughts not concerned with his work, be they ever so serious, such as thoughts of the human relationships involved in his practice, must yield ground and disappear.

The escape to a slower-paced style of life is closed off: for the individual because he would not survive economically; for peoples no less, because any economic stagnation, any slowdown or even a failure to advance in the factories, would bring the danger of crisis, deterioration, and ruin. The machinery of mass opinion—newspapers, radio, cinema, television—must provide guidance for men as they relax from their duties, and must carry for them the burden of all decisions not connected with their work. The very nature of each individual's work accustoms him to react ever more surely to signs, and signs are his guide in every situation. Men need directives, and their need increases the more they obey these directives; consequently they disaccustom themselves increasingly to spontaneous reactions. If the dream of machines doing men's work has now come true, it is also true that men are acting more and more like machines. Georges Duhamel writes: "Let us not forget that if the machine is making its way up to an ever greater likeness to man, the stresses of modern civilization tend to make man sink down to an ever greater likeness to the machine." [13]

Man indeed invented the machine, but this does not change the fact that the inventor's intelligence itself is becoming more like the machine's in that it must adapt itself to ever more precisely prescribed tasks. Every man becomes lonelier, for machines can calculate and work but they cannot get inspirations or identify themselves with other machines. Thus, for all their activity men are becoming more passive; for all their power over nature they are becoming more powerless in relation to society and themselves. Society acts upon the masses in their fragmented state, which is exactly the state dictators dream of. "The isolated individual, the pure subject of self-preservation," says Adorno, "embodies the innermost principle of society, but does so in unqualified contrast to society. The elements that are united in him, the elements that clash in him—his 'properties'—are simultaneously elements of the social whole. The isolated individual is a monad in the strict sense, that is, it reflects the whole with all its contradictions but it is not aware of the whole." [14]

Man's character but mirrors the changes in a society which has not yet achieved peace with itself. Society is forced constantly to change its form and adapt to new conditions. In face of the greatly increased technological powers of the present time, which are fostering within our society an equality of social classes, sexes, and minorities, the less advanced peoples are rising up outside and introducing more efficacious institutions with the help of more or less bloody dictators. The culture of the upper classes, which used to be based on inequality, must now everywhere accommodate itself to the demands of the new mass society that is spreading out from the highly industrialized countries to the rest of the world. The machines are forcing the process of self-justification to

take an irrational form that involves victims, violent reactions, and even the danger of annihilation. There are
nations whose surplus, by reason of the very principle
which motivates them, is being given over, if not to the
luxury of destructive weapons, at least to the fostering of
consumption that is illusory and serves no real need. Yet
even in these nations, despite all the improvements and
despite unimaginable wealth, the brutal struggle for
existence, hardship, and anxiety are dominant. This is the
hidden reason for cultural decay: that men cannot use
their power over nature for the rational disposition of the
earth but must, under force of circumstance and inescapable manipulation, surrender to blind individual and
national egoism. This is why the whole apparatus of
amusement and education, including the human studies,
becomes an empty activity; this is why everyone is looking for meaning. The whole has lost its sense of direction
and, in its restless movement, serves itself instead of men.
Even the inflation which is now becoming permanent is,
despite appearances, less the result of military spending
or even of the increasing share of the masses in the
products of society, than of the maintenance of the power
structure. The fault is not in machines. As outcome of and
further impulse to science and enlightenment the machine
was a factor in the bourgeois ascendancy and points to a
legitimate condition of mankind. The machine indeed
gives a new dimension to productive and destructive
force, to the salvation and ruin of society. But it scorns its
romantic critics no less than the panegyrists of the status
quo who centuries ago condemned experimentation as
the devil's art and today, as realists, are defending the
machine against the "myth of cultural criticism," according to which the machine will enslave mankind.[15] It is
certain that a slowdown or even a failure to advance can

only increase the material and spiritual wretchedness which by means of the machine is not only being prevented from increasing but is even being lessened. The greater man's power, the greater the tension between what is and what ought to be, between the existing situation and reason.

In normal periods of its history modern society has sloughed off much of the barbarity that marked earlier centuries. The individual used to be helpless before a horrifying type of justice which was the hunting-ground of narrow-minded, sadistic judges, and which, with the instigation and help of secular and spiritual authorities, continued down to the French Revolution to cater to the privileged classes and to mob folly. Within the industrial states of the nineteenth century, however, this situation gave way in large measure to a security before the law that was zealously defended by the great writers and the advanced sector of public opinion. The conditions of bourgeois society made possible a freer type of man, and precisely for that reason there was need of an extensive ideological apparatus.

The continuing irrationality of society is increasingly incompatible with the state of our knowledge. The helplessness of men before the opaque whole which they keep in existence is ever more alarming. The "existential" anxiety of which so much is said springs from the same source as our inner emptiness: the fact that life, which at one time was regarded as a flight from hell and a journey beyond the stars to heaven, now seeps away into the apparatus of modern society, an apparatus concerning which, for all the surplus it produces, no one knows whether it serves the promotion of mankind or its downfall. Nowhere does the union of progress and irrationality show up so clearly as in the continued existence of poverty and care and the fear of distress and dismal old age, and in the condition of brutal prisons and asylums in countries with highly developed industry. One has to share the blindness of those who hold the scales of our advanced technological resourcefulness, in order not to be aware that even the inmost characteristics of society depend upon outward circumstances. For his own time Kant had already noted the interrelation between morality and social situation: "It takes more to be a good ordinary man than to be a good prince. If the former is not exceptionally bad, he is already good." [16] Correspondingly, we may add, someone on welfare today needs twice as much strength as a man with a secure job, if he is to be morally and spiritually sound or even, as they say, "open to the world." Money is paradise.

The return of Europe to a more primitive condition is due to the fact that people are unwilling to contribute much to the support of such thinking as does not serve the machine. In an age of full employment and the constant inflation of prices, thriftiness with tax money is the excuse for letting cultural outlays lag so far behind industrial profits that any functions not immediately connected with the economy and the military, whether they be universities or hospitals and prisons, can for practical purposes lead only the most modest kind of existence. The material and even the intellectual factors needed for improvement are there, but the minds and hearts of men are too heavily claimed already. The veil which the agents of mass opinion—be they the trashy film or the human sciences—throw over reality is now so thick that the unimaginable abyss between the life of the secure magnate and the life of the harried common man is no longer perceived by either. Whatever improvement is made, the great man lives in fear that he may be a little less well off, and he counts himself happy when he thinks of those with a slightly lesser income. To fall back to the next lower rung of the social ladder can mean a totally different existence. The allurements society holds out keep everyone breathless.

The naturalistic anthropology which, according to a (misinterpreted) Nietzsche, offers security against mass society and appeals to nature as conceived in Darwinian fashion has become all too well known in the last few decades. It praises the elite, and on this count can call the ancients as witnesses. Wise Aristotle, after all, desiring to preserve the self-sufficiency and independence of the State, was unwilling to have help extended to everyone without exception, and he required that crippled children should be exposed and that excessive population be prevented through abortion.[17] He in turn could appeal to his master, Plato, who wanted to let incurably sick people simply die. In our own day Alexis Carrel wrote in his much-praised book, *Man, the Unknown:* "We should . . . ask ourselves whether there are not inconveniences attached to the great decrease in the death rate during infancy and youth." [18] "Although physicians, educators, and hygienists most generously lavish their efforts for the benefit of mankind, they do not attain their goal. For they deal with schemata containing only a part of the reality." [19] He is averse to blindly accepting all the advances of science and gives his own prescription: "to develop the strong." [20] He does not say who the strong are, though they are presumably those who possess economic and political power, the magnates and the dictators. Such expedients, however, are characteristic of the very society they scorn since the so-called strong live off the fact that the others are isolated and easily influenced by suggestion.

In the last analysis, the anthropologists, whose thinking is focused on strength and power, conceive the history of mankind as ever threatening to degenerate into a history of nature. Man is the rapacious race, more brutal than any previous beasts of prey; he preserves himself at the expense of the rest of nature, since he is so poorly outfitted by nature in many respects. Violence, then, is the only principle that can form and preserve the human community. For, says a modern anthropologist, the preservation of its own existence is the primordial meaning of life for any people, as history shows. These naturalistic anthropologists think of themselves as carefully moving within the ambit of experience and sticking to an analysis of facts or events which are accessible to everyone or verifiable by everyone. Unwittingly, however, they elevate facts, and especially man as a force in nature, into a norm, and preach the brutality to which society gravitates without any urging.

Philosophy is forbidden recourse to this kind of remedy. Moreover, it fails to do justice to the reality as positively conceived, whenever it tries to define it. It can profess its allegiance to a possible positive solution only by denouncing the conditions which make such a solution impossible. It agrees with the positivistic anthropologies that up to now the war of man upon man has indeed been characteristic of the race. But insofar as philosophy reflects on the historical process, it must, like theology, insist on the negative side of that process, the gruesomeness and injustice of it all. Philosophy shows men to be weak in the face of their own society, their economy and technology, but it may not draw the conclusion that a greater degree of subjugation is the answer. It cannot prescribe how people are to escape from the charmed circle of the status quo; it can only seek to give the charm a name.

There is no question, then, of telling men how they are to act in order to halt the withering away of the human. It is folly, after all, to think that we can break off the hazardous developments in technology, family life, and all human relationships; all these developments are what they now are because of deficiencies at earlier points in the process, and they have, of themselves, the power to liberate as well as to fetter. But perhaps an accurate grasp of what is false in the situation will enable what is true and valid to force its way through.

Insight into the suffering involved in mankind's situation, the situation in which it finds itself today even at the points where it disposes of the greatest power, can finally help to bring reason into human affairs. For events do not seem to lend much credence to the view that men are concerned chiefly with power. In contrast to their dictators, the peoples of the world have in fact gone to war only with great reluctance; if they have not infrequently been keyed up for war, it is because they have overcome their repulsion through some form of rapture. Men are at bottom far less interested in being "authentic" and "real" than in being happy, even if they have forgotten what being happy means. The happy man does not have to turn malicious in order to feel secure despite what eludes him. That is the truth of an economy of surplus over the truth of bureaucracy.

THEISM AND ATHEISM
(1963)

Crimes committed in the name of God are a recurrent theme in the history of Christian Europe. The ancients practiced torture and murder in war, on slaves (who were supplied by the wars) and as a form of entertainment: the *circenses*. But in spiritual matters the emperors were relatively tolerant. If the Christians were singled out as scapegoats, it was because they did not yet at that time place the state above all else and still recognized something higher than the empire. But since Constantine in his unscrupulous way singled out Christianity from among the existing religions to fill in the cracks in his crumbling empire and elevated it to the state religion, Europe has stood under the sign of that doctrine and betrayed it again and again. If the words of the founder, his recorded will, his precepts had been put in practice instead of being interpreted by the scholars, neither the unified Christians of the middle ages nor the disunited Christians of the modern period would have had their splendid careers. Whatever teachings could have been taken over from the Old Testament, glory in battle was no part of it. Under the heathen emperors, the commandment to render unto Caesar what was Caesar's could bring Christians into conflict with the state and, when they rightly refused to observe it, to the cross. But the Christian emperors would have undertaken no wars of conquest, they would have named no tribunals to punish those who had offended against them. The victorious course of Christianity since Nicaea and especially since Augustine, which was not unlike the expansion of Buddhism since the reign of Asoka, sealed its pact with that worldly wisdom which it had originally professed to renounce. Its readiness for fanaticism, without which its ascendancy would have been unthinkable, testified to a secret and indomitable hatred for that attitude of mind for which its founder had earlier been put to death.

Initially, when the Christians themselves were the persecuted, the divinity appeared to them as a guarantor of justice. There was to be no more suppression in the world beyond, and the last would be the first; it was for the sake of heaven and not because of hell, out of hope and not for fear that the martyrs and their disciples professed their faith. Suppression, even death under torture, was but a transition into eternal blessedness; apparently inescapable conditions were but a moment of false defeats or triumph. All were the likeness of the divinity, even the lowest, and especially the lowest. The man at the stake, on the gallows, on the cross was the symbol of Christianity. It was not the ruling order of the time which determined who were to be the first; the prison and the gas chamber were at least no further from the followers of the divine delinquent than headquarters. If the barbarian masters, the men of quick decision, the generals and their confidants were included in the divine love, it was because of their poor souls. The pact concerned first of all those who were poor in spirit, those whose lives were not primarily oriented toward riches, power, affairs of state, or even towards prestige. In the first centuries of the Christian era, when the self-confidence of the senate and the people was shaken by the aspirations of the tribes outside and the resulting growth of barbarism inside, the gospel of a goal beyond this world gave a new meaning to the lives of the masses, enslaved and unruly under their masters. If it was possible for the primitive Christians to follow the gospel without unconscious resistance, it was because they knew nothing except that heaven was open to them. But the closer their doctrine came to gaining absolute power, the more it had to conform to the requirements of self-preservation under existing conditions, to come to terms with the law of this world—though its main idea had been the relativity of this law—and to conclude the pact it has kept ever since. Darkness gained in importance. As evil became increasingly necessary for it to carry out its plans for this world, hell became increasingly important to it in its thinking of the world beyond.

Theology has always tried to reconcile the demands of the Gospels and of power. In view of the clear utterances of the founder, enormous ingenuity was required. Theology drew its strength from the fact that whatever is to be permanent on earth must conform to the laws of nature: the right of the stronger. Its indispensable task was to reconcile Christianity and power, to give a satisfactory self-awareness to both high and low with which they could do their work in a corrupt world. Like the founder, who paid the price for refusing to show any concern for his own life and was murdered for it, and like all who really followed him and shared his fate or at least were left to perish helplessly, his later followers would have perished like fools if they had not concluded a pact or at least found a *modus vivendi* with the blood-thirsty Merovingians and Carolingians, with the demagogues of the crusades and with the holy inquisition. Civilization with its tall cathedrals, the madonnas of Raphael and even the poetry of Baudelaire owes its existence to the terror once perpetrated by such tyrants and their accomplices. There is blood sticking to all good things, as Nietzsche remarked whose sensitivity was unsurpassed even by a saint. If the great had taken the conflict of Christianity and Christendom as seriously as Kierkegaard did in the end, there would exist no monument of Christian culture. Without the artful patchwork of scholastic theology, neither the works of pro-Christian nor of anti-Christian philosophy would have come into being, nor the struggle for human rights, which found in John XXIII a late high-minded spokesman, nor the remote village with its old church, which was at first allowed to remain intact by the traffic, the sign of a more advanced civilization, in its barbaric and at the same time benevolent manner. Building on the foundation of enlightenment and renewal which had been laid by church fathers, Pelagians, and gnostics against the superstitions of a decaying antiquity, the Scholastics developed the view of the world on which the freemen of the middle ages organized their government and established their cities. The combination of acuteness and precision, knowledge and imagination to be found in the Summas rivals the interpretations of the Torah which have been admired and disparaged as products of the Talmudic spirit. Scholasticism signifies the great age of theology. But while its comprehensive system lent ideological support to a relatively static society, it could not in the end prevent the dissolution of Christian unity.

Scholasticism lived on its inheritance from classical philosophy. Eternal ideals, which are supposed to reveal themselves to the mind like numbers, formed according to it the intellectual structure of reality. Scholastic wisdom was accepted by all believers as an interpretation of revelation, as knowledge of the world, of the temporal and eternal, of past and future. The lord and the saints were enthroned on the highest plane. Above the earth dwelt the angels and the blessed. Then came spiritual and secular dignitaries, lords, freemen and serfs. The ladder of nature stretched into the darkness of non-living things, and at the bottom was the place of the damned. Men had a picture of the universe in which divine and natural knowledge, divine and natural laws were one. In spite of predestination and grace, a man's future in other regions was largely determined by his conduct on earth which had implications beyond the moment. Each man's life had a meaning, not just the lives of the prominent. The political divisions led to the disappearance of the belief in eternal concepts, in the harmony of natural and supernatural knowledge, and in the unity of theory and practice which the Scholastics had in common with the Marxists, though the former glorified the continuation of existing conditions and the latter their transformation. In the end the medieval order was set in motion not only by wars, but as a result of the widening of the world, through economic activity, the misery of the masses, inflation, the beginnings of modern science and the backwardness of the religious professions. The educated reacted with scepticism and humanism, and the threatened powers with a religious renewal. The reformers, who had been preceded by the nominalists, the followers of Cusa and by others, renounced the system as a way of rationalizing the union of Christianity and worldliness. The opposition was all too apparent. They acknowledged it and made it the central part of their teaching. The Protestant way of reconciling the commandments of Christ with those human activities that appealed to them was to declare any reconciliation to be impossible. Nothing could be said, either about the will of God or about the right order of things, which would set up a general connection between the two. Knowledge and science were concerned with transitory things in a transitory world. Luther hated Scholasticism, theories of eternal relations, systematic philosophy, "the whore Reason." The view that men could justify their private or collective lives in theological terms and determine whether they were in harmony with the divine seemed to him sheer pride and superstition. Even though he judged Christians to be high above other men, especially Jews and Turks, his final judgment about right action remained suspended. In the end nobody knew what good works were—the church as little as a secular board of censors. Luther's verdict against theological speculation, which anticipated Kant's limitation of metaphysical speculation, left reason free to roam this vale of tears—in empirical research, in commerce, and especially in secular government. The interest of the individual and the state became the criterion of action in this world. Whether the troops waded in the blood of peasants who had risen from hunger, or whether a man sacrificed himself out of political blindness to share his last bread with them, one action was as "Christian" as the other, provided each agent sincerely believed that he was following the Word. The Reformation introduced the era of civil liberty. Hate and treachery, the "scab of time," had its origin in the inscrutable counsels of God, and would remain till the end of pre-history, till "all enemies of the Word have become like dung in the street." [1] The idealist philosophers in Germany, who outdid the classics of liberalism in England in their glorification of progress, came to regard the ruthless competition between individuals and nations as the unfolding of the absolute spirit. God's ways

are peculiar. His Word stands: We must love our enemies. But whether this means burning the heretic and
the witch, sending children to work before they can read,
making bombs and blessing them, or whether it means
the opposite, each believer has to decide for himself without even suspecting what the true will of God might be.
A guiding light, though a deceptive one, is provided by
the interest of the fatherland, of which there is little mention in the Gospels. In the last few centuries, an incomparably greater number of believers have staked their
lives for their country than for the forbidden love of its
enemies. The idealists from Fichte to Hegel have also
taken an active part in this development. In Europe, faith
in God has now become faith in one's own people. The
motto, "Right or wrong, my country," together with the
tolerance of other religions with similar views, takes us
back into that ancient world from which the primitive
Christians had turned away. Specific faith in God is growing dim.

Theology was able to adapt itself to the triumphs of the
new science and technology in the last few centuries. In
those European countries which had resisted the Reformation, especially in France and Italy, the intellectual
and political struggles produced a form of life in which
the consciousness of civil liberty was allowed to flourish
while Christianity in its traditional form was able to retain a place in connection with it. There the social forces
which had found expression in the Enlightenment were
able to assert themselves in political reality, whereas in
the German states they were confined to the subjective
realm, to the benefit of romantic poetry, great music and
idealist philosophy. Here the way to bliss led again
through faith, through the idea. Similarly religion,
whether Catholic or Protestant, survived the nineteenth

century as an element of bourgeois life, even though it changed its role. Much of the credit for its survival belonged to the militant atheists. Even when the great atheists did not themselves suffer martyrdom for their beliefs like Bruno and Vanini, it was so obvious that the antithesis—their radical or not so radical departure—was inspired by the thesis—the spirit of the Gospels—that they were far more capable of deepening the interest in religion than of extinguishing it. Voltaire, the foremost among them, was still so generous as to let theism pass, and his work remained as foreign to the general consciousness as Goethe's, which resembled his. The popular figure of atheism, metaphysical materialism, was too barren to become a serious threat to Christianity as long as it lacked a dialectical and idealistic—or in reality, a utopian and messianic —theory of history. As long as government was not yet in control of everything, from the co-operation of political and economic forces in commerce and industry to the conduct of one's private life—the struggle with solitude which is called "spare time"—preaching the love of God and trust in His guidance continued to be the better way. The Absolute of the theologians was incomparably more effective in providing consolation, incentive and admonition than any concept which the philosophical materialists had to offer. True, their critique of theism sounded plausible enough. "It has always been in the womb of ignorance, fear and misery that men have formed their first conceptions of the divinity," [2] writes Holbach in his *System of Nature*, the bible of eighteenth-century materialism. This shows that those teachings "were either doubtful or false and in any case deplorable. In fact, whatever part of the globe we look at, whether the icy regions of the North, the torrid ones of the South, or the most moderate zones, we find that people everywhere have trembled and, as a result of their fears and their misery, either created their own national gods or adored those brought to them from elsewhere. It is ignorance and fear which have created the gods; conceit, passion and deceit which have adorned and disfigured them; it is weakness which adores them, credulity which nourishes them, and tyranny which supports them in order to profit from the delusions of men." So much for the materialist's account of the origin of religion. In place of the rejected divinity they offer Nature. "Nature," continues Holbach at a later place, "tells the pervert to blush at his vices, at his shameful inclinations, his misdeeds; she shows him that his most secret disorders will necessarily affect his happiness.... Nature tells the civilized man to love the country in which he was born, to serve it faithfully, to enter with it into a community of interests against all those who might try to harm it." [3] In the name of Nature the enlightened Holbach calls for the defense of one's country not only against external enemies but against internal tyrants. But what does he mean by "Nature"? There is nothing outside her; she is one and all at once. Man shall discover her laws, admire her inexhaustible energy, use his discoveries for his own happiness, and resign himself to his ignorance of her last, her ultimate causes which are impenetrable. With his whole being man belongs to her. [4] The abstract entity which, according to such materialists, forms the basis of right conduct is as indeterminate as the *Deus absconditus* of the Protestants, and the promise of happiness in this world is as problematical as bliss in the next, which is extremely uncertain. The naturalistic doctrine agrees with the theological doctrine it opposes in identifying what is most permanent and powerful with what is most exalted and worthy of love—as if this were a matter of course. In their fear of death men turn to the One, eternal and immortal—which is their own wishful thinking hypostatized—as if in obedience to a superior power. The ancient materialists were still inclined to stop with a plurality of atoms; the worshippers of Nature, like the pantheists, ontologists and theologians, will hear of nothing less than the One. But Nature does not say anything, as little as Being, which has been tried recently and which is supposed to deliver its oracles through the mouths of professors. The place of God is taken in each case by an impersonal concept. The Scholastics had already depersonalized the humanity and individuality of the murdered Jesus by multiplying them as it were into the Oneness of God. The *ipsum esse*, the true identity of the divinity, his humanity could hardly be distinguished any longer from the radiant Being of the neo-Platonists, because of the ceaseless interpretation of being and being-in-the-world—the unity of essence and existence— in which all differences disappeared. When they build a system, theists and atheists alike posit an entity at the top. The dogma of a Nature which can speak and command— or at least serve as a principle for deducing moral truths— was an inadequate attempt to go along with science without giving up the age-old longing for an eternal guideline. But nature could only teach self-preservation and the right of the stronger, not for example liberty and justice. The liberal bourgeois order was always forced to pursue non-rational interests. Traditional institutionalized religion was still in a far better position to arouse these interests than atheism of whatever kind. The French materialists of the eighteenth century and especially the so-called "free-thinkers" and the pale monists of the nineteenth century were only a passing threat to Christianity.

The upheavals which began with the present century —the era of world wars, of nations awakening all over the globe, of stupendous population growth—can only be compared with the decline of antiquity or the middle ages. Christianity and theism in general are far more seriously called in question than in the *Siècle des Lumières*. In the nineteenth century, individual advancement depended in relatively wide areas on general education, initiative, responsibility and foresight. In a changing economy, the decisive qualities are now versatility, ability to react precisely to stimuli, specialized skill, reliability. We are witnessing a rapid decline in the importance of highly differentiated and independently acquired attitudes, along with a decline in the role of those qualities and of the family which produced them. But qualities which lose their social utility become obstacles, the marks of the provincial, of backwardness. These changes in the psychological structure are part of a comprehensive process in which political and religious institutions are also involved. Democracy is being undermined, at least as Locke and Rousseau conceived it and as it was still functioning under the French Third Republic and even in imperial Germany: as a conflict between the different commercial, industrial and agrarian interests of independent groups. (The relationship between workers and employers formed as it were a surd which could not be expressed in parliament.) There has been a radical change in the character of the deputies, in their relationship to their party, in their ability to form their own independent judgments on the questions under debate. When faced with important matters of state, especially in foreign policy and even more so in case of conflict, the clumsy democratic apparatus calls for its own transformation into a fast and efficient instrument operated by strong men. Theology had to adapt not only to structural changes in the social mechanism and to the related transformation of the family and the individual; a powerful enemy, called "communism" by friend and foe alike, sprang up at the same time. This threat, which concerns not only religion but civilization as such, comes not so much from the theory of Marx and Engels which is itself among the greatest achievements of civilization. Dialectical materialism was, moreover, quickly transformed into a mere ideology, like the bourgeois Enlightenment after its victory in the French Revolution and like theistic religions wherever they come to power. Much more important is a social mechanism which is also operative in other countries where it is about to integrate religion completely with the state, and which ensures that the only serious interest transcending the horizon of individual self-preservation is collective power, the rule of one's own nation or supra-national block. National socialism was a case in point. It had no longer any need of Christianity and felt it as a threat in spite of mutual concessions. Anybody, whether theist or atheist, who did not belong without reservations was an enemy of the national atheism. Even today the Third Reich—the savage collective will to power—tends everywhere to suppress the thought of another Reich and to achieve thereby what the *civitas terrena*—in spite of the gruesome deeds it committed in the name of the *civitas Dei* throughout history —was unable to accomplish earlier because of its backward technology: a world without shelter.

The changes with which Catholics and Protestants alike are trying to meet the threat in the developed countries are no less far-reaching than the most fundamental changes in the history of theology. Rome these days (May 1963) is both progressive and conservative. The new spirit seeks to improve the lot of the workers, to give them a share of the wealth in free countries and to liberate them from brutal suppression under backward dictatorships. Social movements are judged without hatred even when they derive from an anti-religious doctrine. Who could deny, we are asked in *Pacem in terris*, the papal encyclical, "that something good and worthy of recognition is to be found in such movements, as long as they conform to the law and order of reason and take into account the just demands of the human person?" [5] The inevitability of social change is being acknowledged and affirmed. But tolerance of social progress is combined, by internal necessity, with the endeavor to salvage as many middle-class virtues as possible and to build them into the new order even at the risk of making quick adaptation to existing conditions impossible. It is by remaining within the tradition while giving it a new sense that the Church is trying to take an active part in shaping society. Its efforts to keep up with the times appear modest when compared with the conclusions that Protestant theologians have already drawn. The latter have eliminated the possibility of any conflict not only with science—which science in its positivistic form has been avoiding in any case—but even with all moral principles, no matter what their content may be. Further, the assertion that God really exists as a person or even as a trinity—not to mention the other world—is true only in a mythical sense. According to a popular work, *Honest to God*, by John Robinson, an Anglican bishop, which is now being debated in several countries, the whole conception of a God who "visited" the earth in the person of His Son is as mythical as the prince in the fairy tale. The "supernatural scheme" which includes for example the Christmas story and corresponding legends can, we are told, survive and take its place as a myth "quite legitimately." [6] The only reason why it ought to survive is that it points to the spiritual meaning of our lives. Robinson is only putting into simpler words the thoughts of Paul Tillich and other philosophical theologians: The stories of the Bible are symbolic. When the New Testament tells us that God was in Christ and that the Word was God, this only means according to Robinson that God is the ultimate "depth" of our being, the unconditioned within the conditioned.[7] The so-called "transcendent"—God, love, or whatever name we might give it—is not "outside" but is to be found in, with and below the Thou of all finite relationships as their ultimate depth, their ground, their meaning.[8] But if we must talk of ultimate, then Schopenhauer was closer to the truth when he denounced it in each creature as the instinct for self-preservation, the will to be and to be well. However well-intentioned, the bishop's words turn out to be mere verbiage, unctuous words which to German ears are nothing but well-worn clichés. And even though theism is to be sacrificed for an anti-dogmatic attitude, the rejected view is being presupposed in a perfectly naive way. Truth—eternal truth outlasting human error—cannot as such be separated from theism. The only alternative is positivism, with which the latest theology is in accord irrespective of contradictions. On the positivist view, truth consists in calculations that work, thoughts are instruments, and consciousness becomes superfluous to the extent that purposive behavior, which was mediated by it, merges into the collective whole. Without God one will try in vain to preserve absolute meaning. No matter how independent a given form of expression may be within its own sphere as in art or religion, and no matter how distinct and how necessary in itself, with the belief in God it will have to surrender all claim to being objectively something higher than a practical convenience. Without reference to something divine, a good deed like the rescue of a man who is being persecuted unjustly loses all its glory, unless it happens to be in the interest of some collective whole inside the national boundaries or beyond them.

While the latest Protestant theologians still permit the desperate to call themselves Christians, they subvert the dogma whose truth alone would give their words a meaning. The death of God is also the death of eternal truth.

Having retreated to their last position, Protestant theologians, unconscious of this philosophical dilemma, try to rescue the idea that the life of each individual has its own meaning. It is essential for life in this world to mean something more than this world. What more? Their answer is: Love. The reason why love remains to determine what cannot be determined is obviously the memory of the Christian heritage. But love as an abstraction—as it appears in recent writings—remains as obscure as the hidden God whom it is supposed to replace. If its consequences for thought and action are not to be left entirely to chance, it is essential that the various implications contained in this principle be made explicit. The meaning of the concept would become apparent if it were explicated in the form of a theory of reality—of those real situations in which it should be tested. One would then deduce from the concept of Christian love how the world appeared today within its horizons, in which direction it could work within society, and especially, to what extent it would have to be negated to be able to express itself—not to speak of finding the strength to assert itself. As the theory was being developed, it would in turn affect the principle behind it by defining it more fully and by modifying it. Even the will to eradicate all hunger and injustice is still an abstraction, though it is already more concrete than empty talk about values, eternal meaning and genuine being. The idea of a better world has not only been given shape in theological treatises, but often just as well in the so-called "nihilistic" works—the critique of political economy, the theory of Marx and Engels, psychoanalysis—works which have been blacklisted, whether in the East or in the West, and provoked the wrath of the mighty as the inflammatory speeches of Christ did among his contemporaries. The opposition between theism and atheism has ceased to be actual. Atheism was once a sign of inner independence and incredible courage, and it continues to be one in authoritarian or semi-authoritarian countries where it is regarded as a symptom of the hated liberal spirit. But under totalitarian rule of whatever denomination, which is nowadays the universal threat, its place tends to be taken by honest theism. Atheism includes infinitely many different things. The term "theism" on the other hand is definite enough to allow one to brand as a hypocrite whoever hates in its name. When theism adopts eternal justice as a pretext for temporal injustice, it is as bad as atheism insofar as it leaves no room for thoughts of anything else. Both of them have been responsible for good and evil throughout the history of Europe, and both of them have had their tyrants and their martyrs. There remains the hope that, in the period of world history which is now beginning, the period of docile masses governed by clocks, some men can still be found to offer resistance, like the victims of the past and, among them, the founder of Christianity.

Even though Catholics and Protestants are nowadays both on the defensive, theism is again becoming an actual force in the period of its decline. This follows from the very meaning of "atheism." Only those who used "atheism" as a term of abuse meant by it the exact opposite of religion. Those who professed themselves to be atheists at a time when religion was still in power tended to identify themselves more deeply with the theistic commandment to love one's neighbor and indeed all created things than most adherents and fellow-travelers of the various denominations. Such selflessness, such a sublimation of self-love into love of others had its origin in Europe in the Judaeo-Christian idea that truth, love and justice were one, an idea which found expression in the teachings of the Messiah. The necessary connection between the theistic tradition and the overcoming of self-seeking becomes very much clearer to a reflective thinker of our time than it was to the critics of religion in by-gone days. Besides, what is called "theism" here has very little in common with the philosophical movement of the seventeenth and eighteenth centuries which went by that name. That movement was mostly an attempt to reconcile the concept of God with the new science of nature in a plausible manner. The longing for something other than this world, the standing-apart from existing conditions played only a subordinate part in it and mostly no part at all. The meanings of the two concepts do not remain unaffected by history, and their changes are infinitely varied. At a time when both the national socialists and the nationalistic communists despised the Christian faith, a man like Robespierre, the disciple of Rousseau, but not a man like Voltaire, would also have become an atheist and declared nationalism as a religion. Nowadays atheism is in fact the attitude of those who follow whatever power happens to be dominant, no matter whether they pay lip-service to a religion or whether they can afford to disavow it openly. On the other hand, those who resist the prevailing wind are trying to hold on to what was once the spiritual basis of the civilization to which they still belong. This is hardly what the philosophical "theists" had in mind: the conception of a divine guarantor of the laws of nature. It is on the contrary the thought of something other than the world, something over which the fixed rules of nature, the perennial source of doom, have no dominion.

THE SOUL
(1967)

Anyone who undertakes these days to discuss the idea of
the soul must, in the last analysis, deal with two diametri-
cally opposed conceptions of it: on the one hand, the scientific which acknowledges so-called psychic powers and
functions but not a substantial, and certainly not an immortal, soul, and, on the other, the vestiges of theological
tradition. Research institutes conduct numerous inquiries,
yet I know of no penetrating study, for western Europe,
which aims at determining the precise meaning and degree of vitality that the soul concept has at contemporary
man's various levels of awareness. We may surmise indeed, on the basis of our everyday experience, that most
members of the older generations, except for scientists
and not a few other people, have kept, side by side, both
modes of thought: the empirico-objective and the traditional. Consequently, in varying situations and in varying areas of life (for example, the private and the professional), their internal and external reactions will be determined by the one or the other of these modes of
thought. The more advanced among our young people,
on the contrary, react not only skeptically but aggressively
to the image of a soul as they do to everything traditional.

They are aware of the human need which used to be satisfied by such cultural holdovers, and also of the formalis-
tic lip-service paid the latter today. They feel the contradiction and denounce any effort to gloss it over. The
strictly scientific mind is content to refer to some other
field, in which accuracy is not attainable (such as music,
religion, metaphysics, or cocktail parties), any questions
Youth, on the contrary, responds with deliberate mockery
and exaggerated negation to postulates which only convention keeps alive; such a response represents, however,
an incisive demand for the truthfulness of such principles
and ideas as they are asked to take into account in the
living of their lives.

Belief in the soul may appeal to the various tribunals
of spiritual authority, but it finds dubious support at best
not only in the natural sciences but even in philology and
history. Theologians will refer to the Gospels, for example, in their efforts to prove the eternity of the soul. Yet
it is by no means clear how far, in the original text of the
Old and New Testaments, the meaning of the word we
translate as "soul" corresponds to any of the senses which
members of a modern religious community would attribute to it. I do not dare venture an opinion in the philolog-
ical discussion of this point, but I believe that, apart from
a few isolated anticipations, the conception of a soul that
is separable from the body and outlives it, and the doctrine of man as constituted by two substances, a body and
a soul, arise in a development that is independent of the
Scriptural text.

The assertion that man, unlike the brute beast, has a
soul which enjoys independence of the body, has its roots
in ancient Greece rather than in Judeo-Christian sources.
Among the surprising problems this conception has raised

for Scholasticism we may note, for example, the question
of how the soul, once separated from the body by death,
can be punished in the fire of hell. St. Thomas Aquinas
discusses it in a special chapter of his *Summa contra Gentiles*.[1] When the ordinary reader comes across the words,
"Out of my sight, you condemned, into that everlasting
fire prepared for the devil and his angels" (Matt. 25:41),
he probably thinks of the whole man being thrust into
that darkness where there is "wailing . . . and the grind-
ing of teeth" (Matt. 8:12). Thomas, the Aristotelian, however, speculates that if the soul, which is the vital form of
the body and in turn receives its individuation from the
body, carries a burden of guilt with it when it leaves the
body, it will enter into bondage to material fire. The sin-
ful spirit's punishment, he says, is "to be subject somehow
to the bondage of things which are its own inferiors,
namely, bodily things." [2] Such a soul goes from the human
body to the flames. The Egyptian-Indian conception of
the migration of souls, which passes via Pythagoras, Em-
pedocles, and Plato to the Fathers of the Church, here
exercises an influence on Scholasticism.

Among the early Christians anxiety concerning hell
was still closely identified with anxiety for their own bod-
ies, just as among the martyrs in the Roman arena the
hope of blessedness was closely identified with the expectation that their agonizing death would be a gruesome
but quick, sure, and utterly real passage from earth to
heaven, from a lower realm of space to a higher realm of
space rather than to some non-spatial realm. The dualism
of soul and body that is expressed in some mysterious biblical texts such as Ecclesiastes 12:7: after death "the dust
returns to the earth as it once was, and the life breath returns to God who gave it," became a conscious matter of
vital importance to the Christian world-view only when

the doctrine of God the Lord and his creation, of heaven and earth, and of the origins of human history in man's expulsion from paradise, came into sharp opposition to the new sciences of astronomy, ethnology, history, biology, and physiology. The Thomistic hypotheses were affected along with other Scholastic hypotheses.

The elaboration of theories and systems to ground a view of the world and life that would reconcile basic religious concepts with scientific progress is the central preoccupation of modern philosophy. The Protestant decision to accept the new information as knowledge and the word of God as faith (in the sense not of mere opinion but of a higher certainty) serves the same purpose, and the English mind, already represented by important Nominalist forerunners of Protestantism, has, in essence, remained true to this conviction. The first systematic attempt to justify the thesis of the two substances, spiritual and corporeal, non-spatial and spatial, in such a way that it would be compatible with science, especially mathematics, dates from the seventeenth century and was the work of René Descartes, who begins the history of modern philosophy. The writings of his successor, Spinoza, contain psychological insights of critical importance. As a pantheist, Spinoza had no interest in the personal survival of the individual. In his view, the wise man has no time to waste on such problems. Nonetheless, insofar as thought knows itself to be one with the absolute and permanent, to which it truly belongs, it shares in the character of the latter. Finite beings, taken by themselves, do not form substances but are only ephemeral modifications or waves on the ocean of eternal being. That such momentary forms must pass away is obvious; nonetheless, they do belong to the eternal, and it is the purpose of concrete existence to become conscious of that truth and to correspond to it in thought, feeling, and action. The idea that the soul is one with the omnipresent substance, and the rejection of the empty existence of the isolated individual who idolizes itself as an absolute instead of perceiving itself to be a modality or swiftly passing variation of the true Absolute—these, like the migration of souls, point back to early Indian thought. In Averroes (twelfth-century Islam) and Pomponazzi (fifteenth-century Europe), to name but two, the heretical idea of the union of the individual soul with the world-soul or world-spirit has found intelligent representatives among theologians and offered them its consolation; it continues to do so down to our own day. Hegel's doctrine is not far removed from this kind of annullment—sublimation of the individual.

Leibniz, on the contrary, maintained the idea of the substantial individual soul; in fact he makes it the principle of his explanation of the world. Monads, which are immaterial, spiritual essences, form, in Leibniz's view, the truly real. The lower monads live vague, unspirited lives. Consciousness, spirit, and soul are essential attributes of the higher monads. Perceptions, feelings, thoughts, visual impressions, pain, expectation, and memory are immediately certain, while the spatial world, the universe, however exactly it may be measured, is only the result of conceptual elaboration of material supplied by the senses and, thus, of careful thought on the part of the subject. The hierarchy of monads or ordered realm of true reality is determined by the clarity, differentiation, and spontaneity of each monad. Death is a change in the relations between monads, a separation of structures, and not the end of their lives. Immortality is an essential attribute of the spiritual atoms, be they high or low in the scale, of which being is composed.

I am well aware of the difficulties inherent in such suggestions. I have mentioned these systems only because their efforts to create an image of total reality which will satisfy both science and the theological heritage are evidence of the unrest and doubt concerning the immortal soul that have marked western civilization for centuries now. Whatever the truth these systems may contain, they are not regarded today as compelling acceptance. Like works of art, they are respected as historically significant but not as valid interpretations of life today. Even if reflection on the soul cannot go beyond these systems, they cannot help us in our perplexity. The formulations of the eighteenth-century Enlightenment, on the other hand, are still highly relevant to us.

" 'What do you think of the soul?' " we read in one of Diderot's dialogues. " 'I do not speak of what I cannot know.' 'And of its immortality?' 'If I do not know the soul's essence, how can I know whether it is immortal? I do know that I had a beginning; should I not assume that I will also have an end? Yet the idea of nothingness terrifies me, and so I raise my mind to the Supreme Being.' " [3] There is no other recourse left. "What are you? Whence do you come? What are you doing? Whither do you go?" are questions doubters ask themselves, according to Voltaire (1768). The answer: "You're a thinking, feeling being, but even if you think and feel for a hundred thousand million years, your own intellectual powers will not lead you to further knowledge in these matters. You must have the help of a god." The theists took refuge in God, the unknown; the professional theologians, in their view, only made reconciliation with progress more difficult. The atheists found that theism rests on weak foundations. They could easily point to Diderot's vacillation and to Voltaire himself who wrote in a letter to Count D'Argental: "I like the Swiss captain who before the battle said his prayers behind a bush: 'My God, if there is a God, have mercy on my soul if I have one.' "[4]

Skepticism has continued to spread since the eighteenth century. The theologians, for all their concessions to change, still seek, from an instinct for self-preservation, to maintain the thesis of the immaterial individual soul, but the process of dissolution cannot be stayed. Despite all the lip-service paid to tradition, the thinking that is controlled by science (as popularly conceived) becomes ever more widespread in city and countryside. What still seemed a rather radical outlook in the twenties is basically accepted today. "The thing which is said to be immortal," we read in Fritz Mauthner, "is for contemporary psychology (which gets along without a psyche) no longer a thing or substance or whatever else you call the subject of which immortality is predicated or denied. The word 'soul' and its little retinue of related words may survive for a hundred years or more, because the common speech always contains many relics of religion and similar outdated types of 'knowledge.' Even in scientific speech we are as yet unable to do without the word 'soul,' because it frequently sums up in a single syllable, as in a mathematical formula, a whole treasury of ideas." But the meaning of the word is changing. " 'Soul' is now simply a word for a 'function.' "[5] Nietzsche, who had long been determined to root out the "soul superstition," had already summed up this position: "We have a nervous system, but not a soul." [6]

Decades ago, a well-known pathologist in anatomy declared that in all the dissections he had done he had never discovered a soul. If you objected that he was dealing with dead men, not living ones, a surgeon might tell you that he too had never discovered a soul. Science cannot accept the existence of a reality that can never be perceived by even the most delicate instruments or of something substantial that can remain or depart without betraying its presence. The outward manifestations attributed to the soul or rather to the soul's powers can usually be correlated with physiological processes, especially in the central nervous system, which are subject to investigation and can to some extent now be influenced by chemical means. Moreover, it is now possible to isolate certain material substances which are produced in the organism when the eyes or other senses give rise to wishes and appetites, depressions or feelings of pleasure. Man—heart and brain and all manifestations included—is now taken to be a sum of processes, the conditions for which are, in principle, subject to investigation by the natural sciences. The construction of automated apparatus, the activity of which can not only substitute for some thought-processes but even outdo the latter in speed and precision is a further guarantee that science is able to explain animal and human action without appealing to a substantial, much less an immortal, soul.

I have already mentioned that psychology can do without the hypothesis of psychic substances. The discoveries of experimental and medicinal psychology, as well as of psychiatry and modern social psychology, have generated a concept of psychic activity which yields not only theoretical knowledge but a surprising degree of practical influence on individuals as well as on the so-called masses. Series of happenings, psychic manifestations, attitudes, patterns of reaction, linquistic and mimetic displays, and forms of behavior are observed in order to find rules according to which psychic activity can be explained, predicted, caused, changed, and determined as precisely as possible.

It might be thought that psychoanalysis is an exception to this development. In order to define the concept of soul so as to make it as unobjectionable as possible to science, most philosophers had for some hundred years taken Descartes' course and identified soul and consciousness, soul and ego. Recall, for example, a generation ago, the Vienna School, Avenarius and Mach, the epistemologists and the positivists. When, therefore, Sigmund Freud chose to regard the unconscious (preconscious thought processes, the so-called super-ego, inherited drives and instincts, suppressed impulses, everything included in the Id), which people preferred to think of as a series of physiological epiphenomena, as part of the psychic realm, he seemed to be going beyond an empirico-scientistic conception of the soul. As a matter of fact, however, the conception of the Id was essentially a means of paving the way to much more exact and comprehensive laws than had been possible in the earlier psychology. As in the other sciences, so in psychoanalysis the purpose is mastery of nature, elimination of obstacles, manageable goals, and medicinal technology. Salvation of the soul and cure of the patient are one and the same thing. The aim of psychoanalysis is said to be the capacity to work and enjoy pleasure, and I know of no clearer definition than this of the image of man toward which the development of society is moving, to the extent at least that it is not turned aside by catastrophes. Now that they have some control over their own depraved and harmful drives as well as of their excessive exuberances, men are coming to a more sober relationship with the world at large and with each other. Everything is rationally arranged; the natural instincts, hunger and thirst, the need of distraction and comfort will all be satisfied, as will the sexual drive. Thus the "Great Society" would be brought in being, and life would be so arranged by dint of industrial progress that under an all-provident administration each individual could live undisturbed as long as he obeyed the rules. To infringe these would be a sign of illness, not a crime, and would call for the psychiatrist's services.

I am quite aware that I have too readily made a number of associations. Thus, for example, the simplified idea of psychic health does not necessarily lead to the concept of a totally administered world. Nonetheless, the complex meaning of "soul" at the present moment in history cannot be better described in a few words than by drawing on the most advanced psychological theory.

There are two points to be made here. As the period of liberalism was drawing to its close, the bourgeois individual had, for good or for ill, a great deal of economic free play in making decisions; he was less hemmed in by limitations and rules than today's professional man. Morality and duty therefore played a more important role in society. Civilization was largely a matter of culture, that is, of the inculcation of moral principles. The more fully a man's extraction and education caused properly human behavior to become second nature to him, the more "soul" he was considered to have. Respect for neighbor, sense of responsibility, and capacity for friendship and love were all included in morality as here understood. But as progress imposes stricter limitations on life and regulates behavior more fully, imagination is replaced by purposive systematic procedures, active emotions by reliable reactions, and feeling by reason. "Soul" is becoming, in retrospect as it were, a pregnant concept, expressing all that is opposed to the indifference of the subject who is ruled by technology and destined to be a mere client. Reason divorced from feeling is now becoming the opposite of *Anima* or soul.

SCHOPENHAUER TODAY
(1961)

Arthur Schopenhauer regarded fame with no less detach-
ment than the majority of thinkers who finally gained it.
Public recognition left him so indifferent that when he
partook of it at last he did not even have to belittle it,
either to himself or to others. He could relish the signs of
future veneration and even succumb to the temptation of
agreeing with Seneca's optimistic judgment that fame
follows merit unfailingly. What great respect for the
course of history! Only rarely did the philosopher show so
much confidence in the verdict of a humanity, whose cultural decline he prophetically thought more plausible
than its progress. As if there could be any certainty that
among those forgotten there were no great men: indeed,
hardly any age has demonstrated the universality of for-
getting as clearly as has the present. In spite of our infinitely refined instruments of perception and its communication—not just because of them—only very few of
those are remembered (let alone the thoughts they put on
paper) who in Germany gave their lives in a lone attempt
to put an end to the national disaster. They are of no
lesser stature than their predecessors who were famous.

They are gone. For Schopenhauer, however, justice from posterity was guaranteed, as it were, by that same history which in other respects he hated. Posterity was his longing, his utopia. Nietzsche, his successor, was not thus fooled. "I do not want any disciples," he says in *Ecce Homo*. "I am terribly afraid of being canonized one day. People will understand why I publish this book before: it is to keep them from playing tricks on me." [1] He was convinced that fame is as despicable as the public opinion which awards it.

In regard to one's contemporaries, in regard to "up-to-dateness," Schopenhauer agrees with the author of *Thoughts Out of Season*. One of the prime conditions of greatness, he writes in the *Parerga*, is to have no respect at all for one's contemporaries, including their opinions and views, and the praise and blame resulting from them. [2] What is "up-to-date" in this sense is what happens to be considered valid as a result of the interaction between material, relatively spontaneous, interests and manipulated, secret, and avowed ones. Truth itself, on the other hand, lies hidden, according to Democritus, deep in a well, and, according to Schopenhauer, it gets a rap on the knuckles when it tries to come out. In any case, it has had to hide itself again and again, depending on the state of events, as Voltaire puts it in his allegory. Up-to-date literature, whether conceived with an eye to the market by instinct or routine, serves the established order. Even the notion that opposes it is incorporated, assimilated, decontaminated. The controlled consumption of consumer and cultural goods in a boom period is a match for everything. The late stage of society is in all cultural matters at once cunning and unassuming, modest and insatiable—in this respect similar to antiquity in its decline. It manages to incorporate as its own ornament even criticism, negative art, resistance. The less of a chance the historical situation gives great works actually to inspire human action, the fewer the obstacles to their publication; the more diligence scholars apply to them, the less significant is the effect of their writing.

Schopenhauer's work is not free from such "up-to-dateness." Still, it has suffered from it less than the work of other great philosophers, probably because it is so ill-suited to education for efficiency, even academic efficiency. For that, it rejects too many pet ideas of employees of Culture and Education; it calls neither for Decision, nor for Engagement, nor for the Courage to Be. Schopenhauer does not compensate for the low wages society doles out to the guardians of the spirit by the consciousness of an office that is supposed to be superior to other trades. His work makes no promises. Neither in heaven nor on earth, neither for developed nor for underdeveloped peoples does it hold out that to which leaders of every political or racial hue claim to be guiding their faithful. The apparently comforting title, "On the Indestructibility of Our True Being through Death," announces a chapter that brings despair rather than solace. It is hardly fit to gain friends among the molders of public opinion, except perhaps by the element of denial, for it seems to attribute harshness to existence by showing that existence is necessarily harsh. But Schopenhauer does so little to clothe the negative in a semblance of meaning that he can hardly lead to resignation and conformism.

Yet he saw things too clearly to exclude the possibility of historical improvement. The ending of almost all manual labor, especially of hard physical labor, is something he foresaw more precisely than most of the economists of his day. But he also suspected what could result from such a change. He took technical, economic, and

social improvements into account, but from the very beginning he also perceived their consequences: blind devotion
to success and a setback for a peaceful course of events. In
sum, I might say, he saw the dialectic of such progress.
Not unlike some left-wing Hegelians, who in this respect
contradicted their teacher, he decidedly rejected the idea
of the State's divinity. To Schopenhauer the good state
is nothing else than the quintessence of a reasonable self-
interest; its sanctions protect individuals from each other
and its own citizens from other states. The state is no
moral institution; it rests on force. "At the highest stage,"
he says, agreeing with the founders of socialism, "mankind would need no state." [3] But he saw no prospect of
this ever happening. He deified nothing, neither state nor
technology. The development of the intellect rests on that
of needs. Hunger, the urge to power, and war have been
the greatest promoters of knowledge. The idealistic fable
of the ruse of reason, which extenuates the horrors of the
past by pointing to the good ends they served, actually
babbles out the truth: that blood and misery stick to the
triumphs of society. The rest is ideology.

In the century since Schopenhauer's death, history has
had to admit that he saw straight into its heart. In spite
of all the internal injustice in the various nations around
the middle of the last century, there was still something
like a European solidarity, a kind of urbane intercourse
among nations, a good deal of discretion and even respect
on the part of great nations towards small ones. Since his
death, history has entered a new phase, progressing from
a balance of power to ruthless competition among nations.
Stiffer competition spurred technology, and the arma-
ments race began. Rulers and ministers of state were in
uniform. The anarchy of nations and the arms race inevitably led to the age of world wars, which in turn

eventually resulted in the frantic urge for power in all nations of the world. This was Schopenhauer's prognosis. Struggles among individuals and social groups, domestic competition and concentration of power are supplemented and outdistanced by competition and concentration of power abroad. Schopenhauer shows what it is all about. Material interests, the struggle for existence, prosperity, and power are the motor; history is the result.

Schopenhauer did not offer philosophic rationalizations for his experiences of terror and injustice, even in countries with the most humane administrations. History frightened him. Violent political change which in recent times is usually brought about with the aid of nationalistic enthusiasm, he detested. Not having lived to see the decay of absolutism in its acute phase, with its torture and witch-hunting, burnings at the stake and other methods of qualified execution, he was not interested in a change of system. He would rather, as Goethe writes in the *West-Östliche Diwan,* converse "with clever men, with tyrants" than set out for the dictatorship of the "unified" people in the company of demagogues and fanaticized masses. His hatred of "patriots" springs immediately from the threat to his economic independence, resulting from nationalistic rebellions, but indirectly and theoretically, this hatred is aimed altogether at nationalism and the nationalistic age, which was then beginning. The fanaticism of unity and the violence it announced repelled him. He suffered from the same lack of enthusiasm for the so-called wars of liberation of Prussia as Goethe, and from the same fear of the French revolution of 1830 as Hegel. The great enlighteners of mankind have been very wary of The People as the highest value. Lessing once suggested that men should learn to recognize the stage when patriotism ceases to be a virtue.

"The Nation"—that was the word with which the new forces, opposed to absolutism, stirred up the people. Schopenhauer gave the Germans credit for not indulging, on the whole, in national pride as the English were doing, only one in fifty of whom was prepared to accept criticism of the "stupid and degrading bigotry" of their nation.[4] Of course, later the Germans made up for it all the more, and Schopenhauer was startled to meet in Germany with this kind of demagogy, with "this game of insidious swindlers."[5] For centuries thinkers had denounced mass suggestion and its identical opposite, the inaccessibility of seduced masses, as well as the ferocity of those who have come off badly—all as the result of domination. National pride, like the pride of individuals, is easily injured, even if the wound does not show for a long time. The revenge that follows is blind and devastating. There was a time when fanaticism was a distorted and misunderstood religion. Since St. Just and Robespierre it has taken on the form of exaggerated nationalism, which the strong men in the saddle, when the going is a bit rough, can conveniently call up to rationalize murky instincts. When in an ominous historical moment those in power, no matter how different from one another in other respects, have nothing more to offer to quell the dissatisfaction of the people, they can always let loose on them the peddlers of a nationalistic community, of this mirage of Utopia, and feed them the sugar pill of cruelty. But since historians are not altogether wrong in distrusting generalizations and reflect on differences rather than similarities (as did Schopenhauer) among ruling systems and socio-psychological mechanisms, the reign of terror which broke out in Europe in the first half of the twentieth century, not to speak of Asia and Africa, seemed to be an accident. Anyone who would have dared, in Schopenhauer's day or even at the turn of the century, to predict the course of history up to the present moment would certainly have been decried as a blind pessimist. Schopenhauer was a clairvoyant pessimist.

His fear of the beginning enthusiastic nationalism is a sign of his modernity: to take no bribes from the *Zeitgeist*. He regarded world history skeptically, denouncing it as "the unchanging and permanent," indeed as the unhistorical.[6] Not that he overlooked variations in social injustice, characteristic of various ages and stamping the majority of the people as either slaves or serfs. As to poverty and slavery, he says in *Parerga*: "The fundamental difference is that slaves owe their origin to violence; the poor, to cunning." The reason for this perverted state of society, he continues, for "the general struggle to escape misery, for sea-faring that costs so many lives, for complicated trade interests, and finally for the wars resulting from all this," is at bottom greediness for that superabundance which does not even make men happy.[7] At the same time, such barbarism cannot be abolished, for it is the reverse side of refinement, an element of civilization. Schopenhauer did not remain behind the sociological knowledge of his day—he was faithful to the Enlightenment.[8]

His judgment of the historical situation is based on his theoretical philosophy. Among European philosophers, he pointed to Plato and Kant as his forerunners. What they have in common with him is the gap between the essence of things, that which in itself is, and the world in which men move. What men perceive, what strikes them, how they see everything, depends on their intellectual apparatus and their senses, which in turn depend on the conditions of their biological and social existence. The countryside has a different aspect to the farmer assessing its fertility, to the hunter on the lookout for game, to the fugitive seeking a hiding place, to the pilot trying for a forced landing, to the wanderer, the painter, the strategist, not to mention people of different cultures. And how much more different will it appear to an animal, tame or wild, bird or gnat, not only with regard to color, sound, and smell, but also to form and relations. Just as things in space and time are conditioned by the perceiving subject, so are space and time themselves, which are the spectacles, as it were, worn by all who can see, hear, and feel. Pascal once said that to a creature in an infinitesimal, microscopic world which we cannot even perceive, millennia may pass in one of our seconds—thus a human millennium might appear but a moment to some superhuman being. Empirical scientific knowledge, vital to progress, the technical miracles which are the result of observation and which can increase or reduce life's span, are therefore not truth itself but only the semblance of truth. Plato and Kant described the relation between the two spheres, essence and appearance, differently. To Plato, truth was a realm of ordered concepts, and things were their transitory images. Kant taught that the thing-in-itself—that is, being as it exists in eternity, apart from human or animal perspectives—furnishes the subject with the matter necessary for cognition, with the sensible facts, out of which the intellect, with its ordering functions, produces the unitary world, just as a machine processes raw material into the finished product.

This concept of transcendental apperception, with its power and its "file boxes"—the head-office, one might say, of the intellect—was modeled on factory and business management. The intellect manufactures something conceptually solid out of the flux of perceptions, as a factory produces commodities. Over and above the ordering functions, the categories are, so to speak, the goals towards which they work: the ideas of freedom, eternity, and justice, which show the intellect the direction it must take. That these can be found in reason, that they even constitute reason in a certain sense, is Kant's ground for the hope that knowledge, and with it that which is to be known, will attain truth at a point of infinity, and that truth is not merely a means but the fulfillment.

Kant's subtle rescue of utopia was preceded on the European continent by rationalistic systems, which might be regarded as a series of attempts to save, against losing odds, the perfection of eternal being from the onslaught of the new science that was trying to explore appearance. After the end of scholasticism these attempts continued in the seventeenth century with the help of bourgeois reason. The innate ideas from which these systems develop are halfway between Plato's Ideas and Kant's categorical functions. They claim evidence, and evidence is to guarantee the truth, good and sufficient in itself, vis-à-vis the changing, terrifying reality, which since the sixteenth century and the overseas discoveries was marked by social upheavals and religious wars resulting from them. The need for something constructive, something permanent as the meaning behind all change was the motive power of philosophy. In spite of methexis, Plato had left essence and appearance unreconciled: Ideas were everything, transient things nothing. After the coming of Christianity, the world required justification, whether by faith or by concepts.

Rationalism was undermined by scientific thinking, which had been imported from England, where, thanks to the growth of trade and self-government in the towns, the citizens had slowly adapted to reality in a long drawn-out process; where political consciousness took form as a kind of resignation that accorded with religious consciousness; where convention became a religious matter and religion a civic one, and abstract concepts without facts had long lost their prestige. Conceptual realism had made way for nominalism: facts came into their own right, and concepts were mere names. The Magna Charta asserted itself in the theory of knowledge; empiricist philosophy and the mental attitude attendant on it came to be accepted without much friction. But on the Continent this shift took place as a distinct break. The order whose term had come was here realized only much later, and whatever fails to occur at its proper time occurs with violence. Empiricism and the materialism related to it imply criticism, not only of the dominant philosophy and the original perfection of things which it had proclaimed, but also of the conditions of the world, of social and political reality. A new vision of the future world replaced the old: a universal rational society. From St. Augustine to Bossuet history had been understood as progress, as the history of salvation, in which the messianic kingdom was the necessary goal. Translating this into the secular sphere, Holbach and Condorcet saw social history as the path to earthly fulfillment. The dualism had remained: the better, future world was the meaning toward which men oriented themselves. The one thing which the empiricism of the European Enlightenment had in common with the rationalism it superseded was that the image of the future was couched in concepts which were as if innate and could dispense with empirical verification: liberty, equality before the law, protection of the individual, property. The remaining ideas that transcended facts, especially those of positive theology, fell before the empirical-sensualistic critique.

Schopenhauer's revolutionary philosophic achievement rests above all on the fact that in the face of pure empiricism he held to the original dualism that had been the basic theme of European philosophy up to Kant, but that, nevertheless, he did not deify the world-in-itself, the real essence. Since the time of Aristotle, Plato's great disciple, European thinking had held to the principle that the more real, steadfast, and eternal a being was, the greater its goodness and perfection. I know of no philosophic dogma as widely accepted as this one. Men were to orient themselves toward that which was most real: being-in-itself. Philosophy deduced the meaning and laws of transitory life from the eternal, thus expressing or implying satisfaction of all strivings and a reward for all good deeds. Only good could result from being at one with the most real, the best, the most powerful. In a more modern fashion, philosophers tried to base hope on human reason, that hope which formerly rested on the authority of the father and on revelation.

This is the philosophic conviction and at the same time the function of philosophy with which Schopenhauer broke. The highest, the most real, the metaphysical being to which philosophers had directed their view, away from the changing world of existing objects, is *not* at the same time the good. Degrees of reality are not degrees of perfection. Looking at the positively infinite, at the unconditional does not teach man how he should act; it is impossible to refer to the authority of being when one wishes a guide toward a decent course of action. The true essence which is at the bottom of all external things, the thing-in-itself as opposed to appearance, is something that everyone can discover within himself, if only he looks clearly enough and knows how to interpret the experiences of his own nature. It is the insatiable desire for well-being and enjoyment, a desire which wells up every time it has been satisfied, and not the reasons the intellect finds for such strivings, that make up the ineradicable reality of all that is alive, of existence altogether. In the struggle with nature and with men, the intellect serves as a weapon by providing rationalizations with which individuals, interest groups, and nations try to accommodate their demands to the moral precepts in force. The intellect is a function of the struggle for existence in individuals and in the species; it is kindled by resistance and vanishes with resistance.

Schopenhauer's theory of consciousness as a small part of the psyche, by which it is used as a tool—not to mention his many particular observations of normal and pathological psychology—anticipates the basic principle of modern psychoanalysis. The basis for his theory is the ever-flowing source of stimuli: unappeasable will. Each breath is followed by a silence that is already the desire for the next breath, and each moment which passes without satisfying this desire increases the need and its awareness, until they finally fade out. Breathing stands for life. So do eating and drinking: those cut off from them must fight for them, and the higher the stage of development of the living creature, the more subtle and insatiable the struggle becomes. Need and endless striving, kindled again and again, make up the content of history and determine man's relationship to Nature. If the air were not free but the result of work, men would fight for it as they do for land, and they could not do otherwise. Today it already seems as though they might actually have to fight for air. If there ever was an era that could confirm Schopenhauer's views, it is the period since the turn of the twentieth century, when reliance on progress was questioned least. For Schopenhauer the good is far more the ephemeral, thought, and appearance, than that which keeps reproducing itself.

Nevertheless he acknowledged himself a man of the eighteenth century. He was bitter toward the profundity of the "facetious philosophers" (a profundity widely disseminated today, too, in our schools and universities), who slandered "the greatest men of the last century, Voltaire, Rousseau, Locke, Hume . . . those heroes, those ornaments and benefactors of humanity." [9] He complained that the venerable word "Enlightenment . . . has become a sort of term of abuse." [10] He identified himself most deeply with the fight against superstition, intolerance, and rationalistic dogmatism. What seemed to him suspect about the Enlightenment, even paradoxical, was the identification of what today or in the future exists in all its power—let alone of gory history—with what ought to be. As the epitome of the good, not even the idea of a future mankind whose members were not trying to exterminate each other, was an adequate compromise for him. He is no good as a reference for the prophets of secular salvation and of even less use to the defenders of the status quo. In the face of theology, metaphysics, and positive philosophy of all kinds, Schopenhauer withdrew philosophic sanction for the solidarity of those who are suffering, from the community of men lost in the universe, but without thereby advocating harshness. As long as there are hunger and misery on earth, he who can see will have no peace. In *Thoughts Out of Season*, Nietzsche quoted with enthusiasm the following passage from Schopenhauer's *Parerga:* "That man leads a heroic life who somehow or other, in spite of overwhelming difficulties and with little or no recompense, fights and eventually wins the battle for what will be of some benefit to all mankind." [11] The more lucid thinking is, the more will it drive towards the abolition of misery; and yet any assurance that this is the ultimate meaning of existence, the end of pre-history, the beginning of reason is nothing but an endearing illusion. The heroic, even the holy life, without ideology, is the consequence of suffering and rejoicing with others, of sharing in the lives of others; perceptive men cannot stop fighting horror until they die. The famous idea that, by devoting themselves completely to transcending egoistic aims, morally great individuals can step out of the cycle of reincarnations has nothing to do with positive bliss. Happiness itself is negative. Even the last utopian escape which his teacher Kant, the greatest German *Aufklärer,* wanted to offer—the idea of the ultimate purpose that human history was to fulfill—was to Schopenhauer, in the face of the horror of this earth, only rationalistic deception; the eudemonistic concept of "the Highest Good" was still more so. Enlightened thought has no need of such illusions.

Basically, the classical idealism of Kant's successors, too, abandoned utopia. In that, they are like Schopenhauer. They regard the discrepancy between the world as it is and as it ought to be as overcome once this discrepancy is canceled in thought. Utopia survives only in rarefied form as the deified subject. The world as it appears is no longer that produced and constituted by men, as in Kant, but instead, as in Fichte, the result of free-floating action or, as in Schelling, the result of self-confirming primordial being. The thing-in-itself is identified with the subject, yet not as the negative but as the unconditioned positive. Hegel saw it as the living concept, the infinite movement, in which an antithesis between thing and thought shows itself as conditioned. But although Schopenhauer hated Hegel, he is not so far from him. The life of the concept, of the Hegelian Absolute, is the contradiction, the negative, the painful. What Hegel calls concept —the system of philosophical determinations that arise out of each other and are in eternal movement—is nothing but the rise and decline of what this system comprehends. The great achievement of Hegel's philosophy lies in the very fact that the concept does not exist outside and independently of what disappears and, as it does, is preserved in the concept. The consolation offered by his "wicked optimism" is in the end the insight into the necessary interweaving of the concepts into the whole, into that brittle unity that is called system. Hegel's recognition of logical structure in the worlds of nature and man, as emphasized in his doctrine of nature and objective mind, is by no means as far removed from Schopenhauer's aesthetic and philosophical reflections as Schopenhauer was inclined to think. Hegel speaks of substantive determination, of the absolute final purpose of world history; ultimately, world history moves towards the absolute mind, the philosophic system towards mere insight into the whole. On the real course of history, on the other hand, Hegel says: "When we look at this spectacle of the passions and see the consequences of their violence, of the unreason associated not only with them but also, and even primarily, with good intentions and just aims; when we see the attendant wickedness and evil, the ruin of the most flourishing kingdoms which the human mind has produced; then we can only be filled with sorrow over this transitoriness and, insofar as this destruction is not only the work of nature but of the will of men, we must end up in moral grief, in a revolt of the good spirit, if such is in us, against such a spectacle." [12]

Decay and permanence, the dying of the particular and the being of the universal, are one. Hegel is far away from Fichte's positive pathos, even farther from his *Instructions for a Blessed Life* which, to be sure, had lost all eudemonistic attraction even for the author of the

Speeches to the German Nation. In the destruction of false comfort, Schopenhauer goes a shade beyond Hegel by refusing to recognize, as the ground for deifying existence, the consistency of a system that encompasses the world and thus the development of mankind to the point where philosophic insight becomes possible. The social whole, too, the institutions in which the mind comes into its own, as in art and philosophy, must pass. The absolute mind adheres to the objective and subjective mind of nations, and their fate is to perish, like any group or individual, like anything finite. Reconciliation, the identity of opposites reached through thought, is no real reconciliation, whether it occurs in the present or future state of mankind. The violent stroke of genius by which Hegel, the last great systematizer of philosophy, rescued the positivity of the absolute by including agony and death in it, fails because insight is tied to the living subject and must perish with him.

Hegel's teaching shows that the positivity that distinguishes him from Schopenhauer cannot ultimately stand up. The failure of a logically stringent system in its highest form in Hegel, means the logical end of attempts at a philosophic justification of the world, the end of the claim of philosophy to emulate positive theology. All these attempts rest directly or indirectly on the idea of the world as the work or expression of true mind. But if the world, in its essence and in its actual condition, is *not* necessarily connected with mind, philosophic confidence in the very existence of truth disappears. In that case, truth can be found only in perishable men themselves and is as perishable as they are. Even thinking about transitoriness loses the lustre of the more-than-transitory. Merely faith remains; the attempt to rationalize it was doomed to failure.

Schopenhauer's thinking is infinitely modern, so modern, in fact, that young people have it by instinct. This thinking knows about the contradiction of autonomous truth and is profoundly irritated by it. Philosophy does not move beyond real history. Young people no longer accept thinking that is philosophically out of date. If an attempt is made to pass over or mask the contradictions in which thought inevitably gets entangled, the young lose faith not only in the truthfulness of their elders but in the whole culture in which they participate and whose shares, for many internal reasons, have in any case dropped in value. Technology makes memory superfluous. The young have little reason left to believe the old and their reference to eternal commandments. They try to manage without them. At many universities in America and even in Eastern countries logical positivism has won out, supplanting philosophy. It takes thought itself as mere function, as business. There is no fundamental difference between the production of mathematical formulas and their application in technology and industry. Positivism presents the result implied in the failure of positive philosophy. We need not worry about philosophic truth, as it does not exist anyhow. That is the short circuit which Schopenhauer's work avoids. He is driven by the passion for truth and, like Spinoza, devoted his life to this passion without making a job of it. But his philosophy gives perfect expression to what young people today feel: that there is no power that can transcend truth—indeed, that truth carries in it the character of powerlessness. According to Schopenhauer, positivism is right against metaphysics because there is nothing unconditional which might guarantee truth or from which it could be deduced. But theological metaphysics is right against positivism because every spoken statement cannot help but make an impossible claim not only concerning an anticipated effect, concerning success, as positivism believes, but also concerning truth in its proper sense, whether or not the speaker intends this. Without thinking about truth and thereby of what it guarantees, there can be no knowledge of its opposite, of the abandonment of mankind, for whose sake true philosophy is critical and pessimistic—there cannot even be sorrow, without which there is no happiness.

According to Schopenhauer, philosophy does not set up any practical aims. It criticizes the absolute claims of programs without itself proposing one. The vision of organizing the earth in justice and liberty, the basis of Kantian thought, has turned into the mobilization of nations and the uprising of peoples. Every revolt following the great French Revolution has reduced the substance of its humanistic content and increased nationalism—or so it appears. The greatest drama of the perversion of faith in humanity into an intransigent cult of the state was offered by socialism itself. The revolutionaries of the International fell victim to nationalistic leaders. A certain state of humanity, venerated as the true one, is an aim among others for which men may justifiably sacrifice themselves. But if it is hypostatized as the absolute aim, then, by definition, there is no authority, neither divine commandment, nor morality, nor even—and I think this is no less important—the personal relation called friendship, which could control it. Every finite being—and humanity is finite—which gives itself airs as the ultimate, the highest, the unique, becomes an idol with a demonic ability to change its identity and take on another meaning. The history of many recent revolutions, in contrast to the theory of Marx, offers frightening examples. Before they seized power, the aim of Lenin and most of his friends was a society of freedom and justice, yet in reality they opened the way to a terroristic totalitarian bureaucracy which certainly does not come closer to freedom than the empire of the Czar. The transition of the new China into sheer barbarism is obvious.

The new idol is the collective *We*. It is not the only one. Insofar as conditional aims or motives for life generally are presented to young people as if they were unconditional, they are met with the scorn of those who have become wise or with mock enthusiasm. They see through the conventionality of arguments for a respectable life that are not founded, as Schopenhauer advocated, on simple common sense and, ultimately, on penal law. Young people can see the unscrupulous practices of moral, adult persons. And just because they accept from their elders only their practical nimbleness but not their pathos, because they understand the Idea only as a set of rationalizations, they have nothing with which to oppose mass deception. If it is expedient to accept it, it would be merely stupid to resist it. Added to this is an unavowed yearning, a feeling of insufficiency, and defiance, which by repeating evil, unconsciously tries to provoke the good, so that it will show itself even if it is lethal. A skeptical generation is no more immune to participation in misdeeds than is one of believers. Instead, their disillusioned life, despite all pressures toward a career, engenders the pervasive feeling of meaninglessness in which false faith has a fertile soil. In order to resist it, there would have to be a longing for that which is different, a longing that would have passed through culture without, however, having been victimized by any of its hardened forms.

Now I can be clearer about why Schopenhauer is the teacher for modern times. The doctrine of blind will as an eternal force removes from the world the treacherous gold foil which the old metaphysics had given it. In utter contrast to positivism, it enunciates the negative and preserves it in thought, thus exposing the motive for solidarity shared by men and all beings: their abandonment. No need is ever compensated in any Beyond. The urge to mitigate it in *this* world springs from the inability to look at it in full awareness of this curse and to tolerate it when there is a chance to stop it. For such solidarity that stems from hopelessness, knowledge of the *principium individuationis* is secondary. The more sublime and the less rigid a man's character is, the more indifferent will he be about how near to his own ego, or how far from it, a given situation is, and the less will he distinguish between such nearness and distance when his work deals with them; nor can he give up his labors, even if they become those of Sisyphus. To stand up for the temporal against merciless eternity is morality in Schopenhauer's sense. This morality is not influenced either—for if it were, it would remain calculation—by the Buddhist myth of reincarnation, according to which after a man dies, the soul, timeless and spaceless, is supposed to find the body that corresponds to its stage of purification. The merciless structure of eternity could generate a community of the abandoned, just as injustice and terror in society result in the community of those who resist. Persecution and hunger dominate the history of society even today. If young people recognize the contradiction between the possibilities of human powers and the situation on this earth, and if they do not allow their view to be obscured either by nationalistic fanaticism or by theories of transcendental justice, identification and solidarity may be expected to become decisive in their lives. The road leads through knowledge, not only of science and politics, but also of the great works of literature.

What Schopenhauer declared about individuals—that they are an expression of the blind will to existence and well-being—is at present becoming apparent with regard to social, political and racial groups in the whole world. That is one of the reasons why his doctrine appears to me as the philosophic thought that is a match for reality. Its freedom from illusions is something it shares with enlightened politics; the power of conceptual expression, with theological and philosophic tradition. There are few ideas that the world today needs more than Schopenhauer's—ideas which in the face of utter hopelessness, because they confront it, know more than any others of hope.

THE FUTURE OF MARRIAGE
(1966)

Anyone proposing to speak on the future of marriage must analyze the present tendencies discernible in the phenomenon of marriage and recall its earlier forms. In dealing with the historical aspect, however, I am forced here to pass over important problems and content myself with brief and highly subjective reflections. I shall not, for example, touch on the divorce statistics, although in any attempt to assess the future they deserve serious consideration.

The image of marriage that was generally regarded as correct around the turn of the century, as well as various ideas connected with marriage (from its holiness to the hierarchy of husband, wife, and children), have long since been relativized by serious thinkers, and marriage is today considered to be a social phenomenon that constantly changes as society develops. At various historical periods the type of society—primitive tribes, food-gatherers or hunters, settled peoples, shepherds, or city-builders —determined whether the woman, the man, or their parents were to be the decisive factor in the choice of spouse and even in the course of the marriage itself. Nomadic tribes of herdsmen were for obvious reasons patriarchal and recognized the sole authority of the head of the family. That authority passed to his son; daughters were disposed of as the leader judged best. The temporal and geographic extent of the opposite way of life, matriarchy, is disputed today as are other phenomena of early history, such as promiscuity and primitive communism. Among a number of peoples at least, monogamy seems to have been a relatively late pattern. Moses, to say nothing of the Patriarchs, had several wives, and the people, especially his relatives, began to complain only when he took a black woman to wife.[1]

As monogamy is but one of several forms of marriage to be found in the world today, so the moral and juridical conceptions connected with monogamy are by no means the original ones, even though they existed, along with others, as early as biblical times and to some extent in Greco-Roman antiquity. Thus Lewis Henry Morgan and others have thought that sexual intercourse between brother and sister was certainly practiced in early human society. Even in some higher civilizations such a relationship was considered meritorious, not criminal. In ancient Egypt where women, at least among the ruling classes, enjoyed high honor and property-rights, a brother-sister marriage was considered to be the best of marriages; it was especially holy when the partners were the offspring of a brother-sister marriage. Even the man in the street felt such marriages to be the most reasonable, and a number of researchers have found that this kind of marriage was "the rule, not the exception." [2] Concerning the Egyptians, Frazer writes that "their Macedonian conquerors [i.e., the Ptolemies] appear, with characteristic prudence, to have borrowed the custom from their Egyptian predecessors for the express purpose of conciliating native prejudice." [3] He finds the reason for incest as an accepted custom in "the wish of brothers to obtain for their own use the family property, which belonged of right to their sisters, and which otherwise they would have seen in the enjoyment of strangers, the husbands of their sisters." [4] A good example of the connection between custom and material circumstance.

Monogamous marriage, but with the exclusion of incest, is the mark of modern western civilization. The family within this pattern has changed however in the course of the centuries. The changes that have taken place in recent decades, and especially the shift from the extended to the nuclear family, are everywhere under discussion. Grandparents, uncles and aunts, cousins, even grown sons and daughters, who used to all live together even in the cities, are now, for the most part, only loosely connected. If elderly widowers and especially widows have no considerable means, then, despite old-age homes and women's clubs, they are usually isolated in a world where marriage is the rule. The nuclear family is but one factor in the spread of the "lonely crowd" and in the loneliness to be found in a nation-centered society. But, before we describe developments in this direction, let us turn to such ideas as have sought to anticipate a positive outcome of historical change, that is, to project a utopia.

The phenomenon of thinkers attempting to give a precise description of the perfect society did not first arise in the sixteenth century when Thomas More coined the word that has since been taken over by the European languages. We find utopias even back in classical philosophy. In Plato's ideal state, for example, there is no monogamy among the upper classes. The men share wives and children, but no man is to know who his own child is, nor any child his father. "If we are to keep our flock at the high-

est pitch of excellence, there should be as many unions of
the best of both sexes, as few of the inferior, as possible,
and . . . only the offspring of the better unions should be
kept. And again, no one but the Rulers [today we would
say 'the administrative staff'] must know how all this is
being effected. . . . The number of marriage we shall leave
to the Rulers' discretion. They will aim at keeping the
number of the citizens as constant as possible. . . . Moreover, young men who acquit themselves well in war and
other duties, should be given, among other rewards and
privileges, more liberal opportunities to sleep with a wife,
for the further purpose that, with good excuse, as many
as possible of the children may be begotten of such fathers." The children of better parents are to be separated from those of inferior parents: " ' The children of
the better parents they [officers appointed for the pur-
pose] will carry to the crèche to be reared in the care of
nurses living apart in a certain quarter of the city. Those
of the inferior parents and any children of the rest that
are born defective will be hidden away, in some appropriate manner that must be kept secret.' 'They must be,
if the breed of our Guardians is to be kept pure.' 'These
officers must also attend the nursing of the children. They
will bring the mothers to the crèche when their breasts
are full, while taking every precaution that no mother
shall know her own child; and if the mothers have not
enough milk, they will provide wet-nurses." [5] To re-
peat: these words do not come from a plan drawn up in
the Third Reich nor from Huxley or Orwell; they are from
Plato's *Republic*, the great philosopher's most respected
work.

In Thomas More's *Utopia*, which was modeled on
Plato's *Republic*, less totalitarian methods are used, for
the author had a truly Christian outlook. More was con-

fronted with the brutal beginnings of industrial society when the poor, who had been chased from their hovels and were roaming the countryside in despair, were deprived of all material aid in order to force them into the unspeakable conditions of the factories. More's answer was to project a homely socialist structure that would preserve something of medieval tradition yet also be adapted to the modest state of productive forces in his day. He took monogamy for granted, but, unlike the later utopian, Morelly in his *Code de la nature*, did not make marriage obligatory for every healthy person. The Social Democrats of the eighteen-eighties and nineties, like the utopians, wanted marriage as part of a properly ordered society. "It [marriage] is to be private contract . . . just as it was down to the Middle Ages. Socialism is not proposing something novel here, but simply restoring, at a higher stage of culture and in new historical forms, what . . . was universally recognized before private property acquired its present domination over society." [6] In More's utopia adultery was severely punished, in many cases even by death, despite the fact that he regarded capital punishment (which he himself was to suffer for his principles) as the law's most wretched confession of failure. Given such drastic laws, every individual would at least have to know what he was doing before he married. In various utopian schemes, moreover, both the man and the woman had the right to see his or her chosen partner naked before marriage. Over a hundred years later, when Francis Bacon described his own utopian vision in the *New Atlantis*, he replaced More's somewhat complicated procedure for arranging this interview with communal baths.

I have perhaps dwelt overlong on the utopians. My purpose has been to provide some detailed evidence that present-day versions of marriage show both ephemeral and relatively constant elements when compared with historical reality and past theories, to say nothing about contemporary literature. The determining factor in all changes, those projected by idealists no less than the real ones, is in the last analysis the function which marriage has within the changing social totality. In the bourgeois era, when birth control was not practiced, the most important function of marriage was the training of the child for psychological, intellectual, and professional integration into society (the provision of material needs, of course, was inseparable from such training). In the achievement of such a purpose the social integration of the married man himself played a necessary part. Voltaire claims: "The more married men you have, the less crime there will be. Look at the frightful records of your registers of crime; you will find there a hundred bachelors hanged or wheeled for one father of a family. . . . The father of a family does not want to blush before his children. He fears to leave them a heritage of shame." [7] As the age of Enlightenment drew on, marriage came more and more explicitly to be regarded as a social instrument.

Like the other factors in society, the relationship between the sexes was in growing measure determined according to a plan and in view of its usefulness for the status quo. In Nietzsche's day, for example, population growth was considered important for military and other reasons. Among the official measures he foresaw were: "Extra taxes and additional military service for bachelors from a certain age on and in progressive degree (within the community). —All kinds of advantages for fathers who bring many children into the world: in certain circumstances, more than one vote;—a medical record to be drawn up before every marriage and signed by the community authorities: in it a number of specific questions must be answered by the engaged couple and the doctors ('family history');—as antidote to prostitution (or as its ennoblement): temporary marriages, legalized (for a certain number of years or months), with guarantees for the children." Not unlike Plato, Nietzsche considers the social purpose of marriage so important that he wants "every marriage accounted for and recommended by a certain number of responsible men in the community" and thus handled as a "community concern." [8] The indissoluble connection between reason and bureaucracy is a law of European philosophy, if not of philosophy as such, no matter how much philosophy may profess to foster freedom. Idealists and materialists alike have waited for history to overcome this contradiction, but history, in my opinion, is tending, at the present time, simply to gloss it over. A life lived according to regulation is presented as freedom; freedom is declared to be a reliable reaction to signals.

The decisive ways in which the form of marriage depends on society's goals may be seen in the social history of Russia during the last few decades. In the years immediately after the Revolution, when the idea of absorbing the now rigidified bourgeois social forms into a higher kind of society was still alive, not only ecclesiastical but even civil marriage (and divorce), and even any official registration were regarded as unimportant formalities. Recall, for example, the book written by Aleksandra Mikhailovna Kollontai, the Soviet diplomat and preacher of free love. Medical interruption of pregnancy, which is still, or once again, allowed every wife in Poland, was originally open to every woman in the time of Lenin. Marriage was losing its significance; the education of children was to be left to the Party, the State, and the organizations set up for the purpose.

But the revolutionaries had deluded themselves. Stalin's so-called "socialism in one country," the veiled admission that a proletarian world revolution was not to be counted on, and herewith the renunciation of what Marx and Lenin had called communism—these put an end to bourgeois freedom and much more to the determination to make that freedom all the greater in backward Russia. The more clearly that military and technological potential became the real object of competition between east and west, the less could extravagancies in other areas of life be tolerated. The liberalist view of marriage contradicted the function of marriage in a state which was fully mobilized and not founded on wealth and well-being. The birth-rate had fallen and the neglect of youth had increased to an alarming degree; therefore the family now became indispensable as an educational agent. There was an end to libertinism. Authority in the family had to be refurbished and, given the new situation, not primarily in favor of the husband. The enormous economic tasks at hand meant a great need of women both in the home and in the factory. The woman had to help both in educating and in earning. Divorce is therefore frowned on in present-day Russia. Marriage and the family are being rehabilitated, far more energetically than in the West, although the process is evidently under the control, in Russia, of the totalitarian State. That control reaches down to the least detail. However, unlike the days when the Revolution first came to power, and unlike the Third Reich, there is less need now for children to spy on their parents. It is true, of course, that such spying has been the usual thing under dictatorships. From Savonarola (and probably earlier) to Hitler and Soviet Russia, betrayal of parents by children has a role to play, since the older generation is initially not to be trusted while the children are already under the control of the new regime. Today, however, the government in Russia can very largely rely on the stabilized and matriarchically oriented family. An article in the *Literaturnaya Gazeta* for December 24, 1965, states: "The mother is sacred and must be treated with great respect by the family, particularly by the father. In the family, the mother's word is law. Her authority is unassailable."[9] Marriage is so well established now that no one who wants to get on in the world even thinks of divorce, which is in any case extraordinarily expensive.

In China, on the contrary, marriage has degenerated at the present time, even though this is the country in which the extended patriarchal family, not least by reason of the highly developed agricultural economy, played a determining role in national and religious life. More even than the changes in work style and the strictly collectivist type of education, the need to control the enormous population growth is responsible for the playing down of marriage. Late marriage, contraception, and abortion are promoted. If reports are reliable, young people have not only acknowledged the government's aims and taken them as a norm, but have even integrated them into their very thinking and feeling. Eroticism is becoming less important, and attention, even in young girls, is focused less on marriage than on the socialist structure: the brigade, the commune, the State.[10] I consider what is happening in China to be in many respects more significant for the future of the West than what is happening in Russia, which is becoming more and more like the West. The fact that the period of individualism is, as it were, being skipped over, as being irrational in today's world; the fact that friendship between individuals is regarded as secondary in comparison with absorption into the collectivity; the pragmatism that has taken flesh-and-blood shape, the purely utilitarian thinking which the Chinese leader be-

trays in every word he speaks—all this is on the horizon
for the West, even though people there make every effort
to avoid admitting it.

Allow me to discuss briefly the three factors just mentioned: the exalting of the collectivity over the person;
the change in human relationships; and the utilitarian
cast of thought. These exercise no little influence on the
development of marriage. The retrogression of individuality does not mean that differences and individual characteristics will disappear. Rather, the more that education in Europe and America is removed from the family
and shifted not only to kindergarten, primary school, and
upper-level institutions but also to the groups, for sport
or other purposes, which are formed in these schools, the
less stimulus there will be to preserve and develop personal distinctions and nuances. The personal psychic
traits which individuals retain become increasingly a hindrance, something peculiar. Acceptable distinctions flow
only from the division of labor and are further stamped
by the particular branch of activity and the life-style that
goes with it. With mounting collectivization and the shift
of competitiveness from individuals to groups, the discussion of divergent political or other convictions loses
its importance for the individual. Professions of allegiance
become identification tags; government becomes an all-
embracing control of society. Instead of voicing thoughts
grounded in world-views, discussions relate more and
more to utilitarian goals, determinable facts, and matters
that can be decided by experiment. The more regulated
a society and the more instrumental its human relationships, the more meaningless does dedication to an individual become. The appetite for sexual pleasure, like the
appetite for food and drink, will be largely subjected to
regulation in the future through advances in chemistry
and will be satisfied without any great differentiation of

means. As the end of the bourgeois era and its specific kind of injustice approaches, the victory of the technological age, which the bourgeoisie brought into existence, is dimming the radiance of the person. The irrational acceptance and eager apotheosis of film-stars, bloody-handed leaders, princesses bent on marriage, astronauts and starlets, and the industrious propagandizing of these in the mass-media (which admittedly have nothing else to occupy their attention) confirm, as it were, that we are seeing the last of the person in the full sense of this word.

The decreasing significance of friendship is a direct result of this situation. Once the individual no longer comes in conflict with other individuals or the existing social scheme by reason of goals he determines for himself and makes of central importance in his life, and once personal initiative plays an ever smaller role in comparison to the pre-determined plans of those in authority, then friendship loses both its practical value and its seriousness. However pleasant it may be, it remains at best a hobby, a leisure-time trifle. The same thing happens to what we call love. When bourgeois marriage was still a relatively thriving institution among the classes which played an important role in its preservation, it presupposed, as far as the children of the family were concerned, that the girl would be chaste and that the young man would woo his bride. For this reason, what was forbidden or an any rate made difficult became, especially by dint of appropriate education, something to be striven for, something worthwhile and fulfilling. Now culture as such, according to so many thinkers from Kant to Freud, is largely the result of sexual prohibitions. If this be so, then love between the sexes certainly depends on taboos. Whether or not love in marriage, where the prohibitions are removed, is not to grow less as the years and decades pass but rather to grow ever deeper depends on particular constellations of circumstance. The mutual interests of the partners must seek their fulfillment amid a cold and indifferent world; care for the children, the awareness that through the children the spouses' own life achieves a transcendence, the development of special experiences and memories that are shared with each other and intensify over the years, all these have the power to transform sexual love into a friendship which is characterized by the sexual difference even when the sexual instinct has abated. With the collectivization of society, however, and its irresistible dynamism that increasingly regulates the whole of life, the breathing space in which to shape an individual human life or special mutual interests becomes more restricted. The higher standard of living in industrialized countries, the improved material situation, and the fact that far more families enjoy the amenities afforded by technology, are paid for with mounting uniformization despite the appearance of increased differentiation.

The less the distinctive character of the individual plays a role in shaping his life and the more the members of the upcoming generation become simply functions in an increasingly planned and managed society, the more fact-oriented, unimaginative, and conformist their thinking becomes. Insofar indeed as the judgment passed on today's young people is based upon the customs of teenagers, their unhampered sexual activity, and their enthusiasm for the Beatles and similar phenomena, the judgment is, in my opinion, superficial. Young people may put no strong rein on their own emotions (which to some extent are a manifestation of their despair) and may have only contempt for taboos, but they are no more irrational than earlier generations; on the contrary, they are more level-headed, utilitarian, and without illusions. They accept what must be accepted; they reject what cannot be proved correct as superstition or trashy romanticism. Even the outbursts from the unsatisfied and undeveloped inner depths show how little room is left for sublimation. Such displays of barbarity would be far less typical if the school-system, up to and including the university, did not necessarily have among its personnel ever fewer educators with the ability to transmit not only factual material and useful or useless data and methods but the something more that used to be called education or culture. Where capable teachers are still to be found, they usually do not want for receptive hearers. The shortage of educators is due to the changed social situation. The contradictory combination of pragmatism and corruptibility in the products of the educational system is a result that is only too easy to understand. The sharp young cynic who sneers at the old songs as tearjerkers often falls victim to slogans wearing the mask of modernity.

A bridge to the old civilization still exists but its piers are becoming steadily weaker. Disillusionment, crass realism, and the absence of any dreams of personal fulfillment are the sign of an interior coldness and find further manifestation in the tendency to give imaginative expression only in quite undifferentiated form to sexual and related impulses. Young people do not have morality in their bones. To the extent that, rightly or wrongly, they experience religion only as something traditional, something purely conventional, they are unable to understand why (if they can escape the police and the criminal courts) violence and cruelty should not be perfectly acceptable forms of gratification. Nationalism, as a substitute religion, may lead to the point in totalitarian countries where a fellow countryman is at least respected until he is called a traitor. In western civilization, though there are exceptions, the earlier religions focused on the collectivity have not yet been wholly replaced by a nationalism of the left or the right (the two are in fact really identical). Meanwhile, the idea of the individual immortal soul, which at one time was the ground for respect of neighbor and a belief in a personal destiny, has lost its power among the majority of young people.

You already have an indication of what I think the future of marriage to be. However long the bourgeois forms of marriage may last, the awareness of a union that is unique in each case, the high significance of the family name, and the will of the partners to create a life peculiarly their own and, if possible, to give that life a permanence through their children, are now passing away. The older, individualistic categories of thought are losing their meaning because of the new awareness of dependence on society and the realization that the service of social goals is more important than the achievement of personal goals; in short, because of adaptation to society as it now is. The equal status of the wife, her professional activity, and the much speeded-up emancipation of the children have already effected a change in the atmosphere of the home. It is not rare for American fathers to feel left behind by their children. Like life generally, marriage is on its way to becoming more rational, utilitarian, and prosaic.

To reject the development is too simplistic a response. For it is not only by reference to the new deity, the collectivity, that marriage is changing its meaning; even in countries where liberal principles still prevail in large measure, the nineteenth century ideal of marriage is proving to be no longer adequate. I am thinking here of the Scandinavian countries, and especially Sweden. Yves de Saint-Agnes speaks of a "sexual revolution" occurring there.[11] Premarital sexual relations and their consequences are not regarded as immoral in Sweden; moreover, marriage is becoming difficult for material reasons (for example, the housing shortage). Even the majority of people in the Church there has come to terms with free love as it has with many other contemporary phenomena. The child of unwed parents is not regarded as illegitimate but as natural, and before the law enjoys full equality with the offspring of a marriage. Schoolbooks tell children that there are families with a married couple at the head, and other families consisting only of mother and child. The social worker and other functionaries of the welfare state to a large extent relieve the woman, and even the normal family, of care for the child. Promiscuity among the young keeps step with the propaganda for contraception and has become widespread, though not more so than venereal disease. Freedom has reached the point where someone advertising for a liaison partner need not pretend to be interested in marriage or even in what would elsewhere be regarded as a natural kind of association. I know of no empirical inquiry into the influence of this kind of progress on the human relationship as such; I suspect, however, that the new liberalism, like collectivism, is not favorable to such a relationship. For, in both developments, we find the ephemeral, the unique, the transitory, stripped of all its magical charm.

Even more than philosophy, art since the twenties has made the nothingness of the individual its main theme, both in form and in content. The various artistic movements that have arisen since Expressionism, especially Surrealism and, even more, atonal music, have not focused their attention on existent reality; insofar as they retain any reference to transitory things, they do so by negation and by shaping an esthetic unity out of the disjointed elements of the animate and inanimate world. The representation of individual realities has come to be regarded as artistic insincerity and fit only for leisure-time trifling, broadcasting, and photography. I cannot enter

here into the question how far art has thereby passed
judgment on itself and tended to become mere ornamen-
tation. In any event, the development of art has been
anticipating that of mankind itself; in expressing the
truth, that is, the dissolution of the ego, the soul, and all
that used to be thought eternal, it leads to its own negation. Art now functions as a useful constitutive element in
existent reality. Because an immanent law has brought
painting from the critical phase associated with the names
of Kandinsky, Max Ernst, and the early Picasso, into total
abstraction and is now once again guiding it towards a
deliberately figurative style, the most recent work of
painters has become pure wall decoration and is accepted
as such, at least by the wealthy who buy it. The dimension of the absolute is disappearing from an art that thinks
of itself as wholly free, just as it is from free marriage that
is untrammeled by tradition. Abstract pictures are now
simply one element in a purposive arrangement; marriage
that acknowledges no norms is simply an element in a
conformist existence. The process cannot be reversed.
That two human beings should find their happiness and
the meaning of their lives in their mutual and unchanging
fidelity is regarded as pure folly, as is every deeper insight
into the conditioned nature of the person and all that belongs to him; it is regarded as comparable to the attempt
to give eternal value in oil painting to the landscape and
its peasant figures. Works of art, like marriage, buy their
future at the expense of their meaning.

The concrete details of the change we are describing
depend on social and political events. It is not possible
now to foresee how far and long the forms of marriage
now practiced under totalitarian regimes will become
models for the countries of Europe and America, and
whether differently nuanced forms and institutions will
again come into being. I am sure, however, that the au-

thority of parents, and especially of fathers, over their children will rapidly decrease. The father's professional and personal experience is losing its importance; the children grow up more quickly; parental control of youth is becoming ever more difficult. Not only the school (which is now geared, however, to vocational training rather than to cultural development in the proper sense) but the mass media as well (television, radio, film) are in large measure taking over the task of education, since the task is now becoming impossible for parents. If husband and wife are both professional people, the years in which the wife must care for the children are an interruption in her career. Childless people get far ahead of her and she must either begin anew or be left behind and isolated. Thus it is not only the earlier mentioned close bond between relatives that is weakening, but even the bond between parents and children who so quickly reach the age when they can work. The State is already taking this fact into account with its system of social security; it supplies at least a modest measure of the help formerly provided by children to parents no longer able to support themselves. The father is no longer the sole provider; the functions of marriage are becoming fewer. This change affects the importance marriage has in men's eyes today. A good many of the evil effects of the old rigid bourgeois marriage— tyranny of husband over wife and children; the unhappiness arising from the fact that the marital relation, felt to be central, meant a whole series of abnegations—are avoided in the emerging situation; we need only think of the tragedies which were a theme of major literary works at the turn of the century, of Strindberg's *Dance of Death*. The fruits of life will in the future have to be sought much more in other situations than marriage.

THE GERMAN JEWS
(1961)

If I correctly interpret the varied attempts to overcome
prejudice, the chief purpose of them in Germany is to
help people understand the phenomenon of the Jews.
Similar efforts have long been known in other countries
and in relation to other social, religious, and political
groups. These efforts represent an essential thrust of democratic society, insofar as this latter description is not
simply a cynical camouflage for a totalitarian regime but
truly designates a form of state in which the individual is
not persecuted for his convictions, his origins, or the color
of his skin, but, on the contrary, may be sure of having
the protection of the law along with whatever else is regarded as indispensable for a properly human life. In this
form of society religious, political, artistic, and philosophical movements seek to enlist the sympathy of the citizenry, whether out of convinced belief in a mission or
out of mere self-interest.

When it comes to the Jews, the aim is a quite modest
one. The aim is that the Jews should be regarded in Germany not as foreigners but simply as a group of men who,
like other groups, share much with each other by reason

of their history, faith, and destiny, while also have having much in common with the rest of the German people. However, the seemingly straightforward task of overcoming prejudice brings with it certain problems which are not immediately evident and are not created solely by the events of recent years. Is it not possible that a particular group's memories, originating in the experiences of earlier centuries, should have become so embittered as to rupture the unity of the people? May not the spirit of a particular group have become so different from that of the larger entity that the ability (so indispensable in many situations of modern history) to react to internal and external dangers is considerably lessened?

Such questions as these have recurred throughout the period since the end of the Middle Ages, when the European nations were being formed. Even when bourgeois society had won its political victory, it was not so sure of itself that it could accept pluralism and be fully serious about freedom of thought within the limits of the law. John Locke, the very model of a bourgeois philosopher and the man whose philosophy inspired the American Constitution, wanted Catholics and atheists to be excluded from British citizenship. Under the influence of the French Revolution Johann Gottlieb Fichte regarded not only the spiritual hierarchy, the military, and the nobility but also the Jews as a hostile state within the state. Only during the nineteenth century did the bourgeoisie become sufficiently sure that its political inspiration could rise to the historical situation, as to extend tolerance to everything but incitement to violent rebellion. The view that numerous philosophical and theological, political and social denominations could exist side by side in mutual respect sounded the keynote for public life in the most advanced countries, at least for a certain period of time.

Since the twenties of this century, however, the pluralist society has been in decline. It seems that the growth of technological expertise, which initially was correlative with the development of the autonomous individual, had in certain circumstances a different set of effects.

The periods of very intense competition between individual entrepreneurs at the beginning of the liberalist age are now being repeated on a global scale but between collectivities. Economic necessity is spontaneously leading to a far-reaching uniformity, and the process is aided by flushing out domestic enemies. Under National Socialism the Jews, as a supposed racial minority, were destined for elimination; in Russia, where international socialism changed into fanatical chauvinism, the social minority was the victim of mass slaughter.

At the end of the modern age the nation has set itself up as the universal idol in place of the Most High. Nationalism, that is, the superstition proper to the nation, is as opposed to love of fellow-countrymen and of the institutions of the fatherland, and to any free loyalty to the state to which one belongs, as it is to the opposite of nationalism, namely, that cosmopolitanism which, unlike the Enlightenment of old, is so hated today. One result of civilization in time past was the developed awareness of other men with their own feelings and thoughts, their gifts and loyalties, even the specific dangers each represented; this awareness was crowned by a sense of the common humanity of every man. The experience of identity presupposes the experience of diversity, not simply among individuals but also between individuals and the whole of which they are a part. The lessening of this awareness of difference manifests cultural decadence as much as does the lessening of the awareness of unity. Men today are too ready to speak not of "I," as spirit and intelligence require, but of "we," because the latter is more suitable for those who regard themselves solely as members of the national collectivity.

Under these circumstances it rings false in the ears of many today to speak not only of power but also and still more of guilt and repentance. The reason is that repentance is a matter for the individual person; it presupposes that all are citizens and have the right to be different. The concern of the German Jews is that this right should be ungrudgingly recognized.

Everyone realizes that we have no definition of the real Jew any more than of the real German or the real European. In any event, the characteristic trait which we just called an effect of civilization—that is, the belief that various life styles should be able to coexist in a single country and enjoy the protection of the law (provided they do not threaten violence to any other)—is required by the existence of the Jews in countries claiming to be enlightened. The same belief finds expression in the very historical phenomenon of the Jews. We need only glance at the nineteenth century, to say nothing of earlier times, in order to see how the historical vicissitudes of the Jews made them dependent on a pluralist culture. Wherever such a culture was in danger, wherever injustice began to appear in Europe, the Jews were among the first victims. From the time of Moses Mendelssohn there were reforms in the status of the German Jews, and the Jews almost achieved equality in Prussia; but once Napoleon Bonaparte fell, there were serious setbacks. Many reforms were cancelled; Jewish residence in the cities was made difficult, and citizenship almost impossible.

Those concerned for the progress of nationalism were more anxious even than the princes that the retrogression be minimized. When Jakob Friedrich Fries came to Jena

1816, Goethe, who did not like him, wrote sarcastically that "according to longstanding laws no Jew is supposed to spend the night there" and that after Fries' visit this "praiseworthy ordinance would probably be better observed than heretofore." [1] The anti-Semitic mob-riots in 1819 were ultimately occasioned by the activity of politicians like Fries. In 1824 the Jews were forbidden any material improvements in their worship, while in 1834 sermons aimed at the conversion of the Jews were ordered in Berlin. The equalization of rights dates only from a not too distant past.

The antiquated order imposed for so long on the citizenry of Germany exposed the Jews to the hatred of that citizenry. Because of prohibitions against their engaging in agriculture and the crafts, some Jews undertook to handle the business of the hated princes. Consequently, in the first half of the nineteenth century in Germany, as in France at the beginning of the Revolution, anger at the reactionary feudal lords passed over into anger at the Jews. Only toward the middle of the century did the bourgeois order finally triumph, and with it the idea of equal rights and duties for all citizens. It was finally permitted to Jewish women to give birth within Bavarian cities, although, if I am not mistaken, it was in Bavaria that the whole humanizing process made slowest headway.

German culture thus accepted the Jews only at a late date, and it is not surprising that German Jews still carry in their faces the marks of their history. The will not only to carve out a place in German civilization but even to serve it has spread among Jews since the time of their emancipation. The Jewish salons of Henriette Herz, Rahel Levin, and Dorothea Mendelssohn (later the wife of Friedrich Schlegel), no less than the rash of baptisms among wealthy Jews of the day, were symptomatic of Jewish enthusiasm for advanced German culture. But neither emancipation nor assimilation are identity. The specific character of an ethnic or religious group does not depend solely on the conscious principles or the rules for life and conduct which the group may accept or reject. Along with the doctrines proper to the Catholic or Protestant as well as to the Jewish religion, certain patterns of thought, associations, inclinations, and repugnances have developed, and these extend to non-religious matters; the same holds analogously for groups whose cohesion depends on something other than a religious faith. Think, for example, of the German dialect groups: Rhinelanders, Schwabians, or Saxons. What distinguishes such groups from one another and from other groups as well is not simply the dialect, but all that goes with speech: the concrete thought-forms, the gestures, the emotional reactions which have been developed along with the language in the course of history, the ways in which people question and invite, sorrow and rejoice. The child does not enter into all this as a natural inheritance (as a mistaken theory would have it); rather in his earliest years he sees all this exemplified in mother and father and makes it his own. Thus, the otherness attaching to a historically developed set of characteristics affects even the smallest details; the more so, the more highly developed and nuanced the otherness is. Yet this is how it is with all human beings, indeed with all living beings; every man possesses from the beginning the potentialities which are actualized in those who differ from him. To grasp this and finally to learn to experience it is the goal of efforts at mutual understanding between groups. The same applies to the two Christian confessions whose bloody onslaughts on each other lie further back in the past than the recent persecution of the Jews.

The varying Jewish responses to German civilization, into which they were finally accepted as belonging, have thus a twofold source. There is the historically conditioned nature of the Jew, which could not simply disappear once Jews had been emancipated; and there are the idiosyncratic reactions of different milieus to the Jews. (Within human societies nothing serves better than small differences as a pretext for projecting repressed feelings of guilt and hatred!) One Jewish response was assimilation. In this event, the effort to be like the Germans led, if not to baptism, then at least to adaptation in all other respects. Such conscious adaptation tended, however, to overreach itself. Thus many assimilated Jews in the German Empire were just a bit more loyal to the Kaiser than other citizens were, and certainly no less critical of fellow-Jews from the East where people still followed the old ways. They developed an acute feeling for the model which they sought to imitate. We are generally more aware of what we are called to be than to what we already are. People often point to the analytico-critical attitude of the Jew and his partiality for the intellectual professions, but they either do not reflect on the reasons behind this phenomenon or they simply refer to the Talmud for corroboration. They seem to think that the casuistry of the early Jewish rabbis was more subtle than that of the scholasticism through which the European mind at one time passed. As a matter of fact, in addition to the long exclusion of Jews from directly productive kinds of activity, one important source for the specifically intellectualist cast of the Jewish mind seems to be the very seriousness with which the newly accepted Jew took bourgeois society. That seriousness was but the obverse of the assimilative process through which western Jewry passed. Some of the most uncompromising Jewish critics of contemporary society were baptized. So deeply did they identify themselves with the order in which they now shared, that they could not but measure it against their own ideal for it. The relationship between Karl Marx and Jenny von Westphalen, whose father was a privy councillor, and her grandfather a kind of military adviser to the Duke of Brandenburg, or the friendship between Marx and Engels, the industrialist who in his private life did not as a matter of fact take prevalent standards as normative the way Marx did, have always seemed to me symbolic of the historical atmosphere in which the work of these thinkers originated. In any event—if I may digress for a moment—Marxist theory shows far more bourgeois-individualistic traits (which at the time meant highly conservative traits) than the potentates of totalitarian collectivism suspect. Assimilation and criticism are but two moments in the same process of emancipation.

Another element in the process was the formation of liberal Judaism, that is, of Judaism as a confession. Ever since the earthly fatherland won out over the heavenly fatherland, this confession, like others, has been intended solely as a matter of private life. In contrast to Judaism as a principle that determines the life of both individual and society and in large measure prescribes the course of daily life and the relations of Jews with each other, liberal Judaism prides itself that Jewish communities and their members form part of the national state in which they happen to live. Liberal Judaism is a free association of citizens who share certain interests. In orthodox communities, on the contrary, something survives of the ancient life-style which once shaped the whole of community life. This is especially true in postwar Germany inasmuch as the Jews gathered in the German communities are primarily those whom persecution and war has driven to refuge there. Most of them come from countries in which the abolition of Jewish isolation is a more recent event than in western Europe. But participation in the new prosperity has not failed to affect the relation even of such people to their cultural tradition. Among them, too, the transformation of religion into confession is proceeding apace.

In addition to assimilation to the life-style into which Jews are accepted, there is a radically different reaction to the proferred equality. It is to be found not in orthodoxy nor in critical liberalism but in the new Jewish-style nationalism proper to the Zionist movement. Unlike the critico-negative spirit which, down to Gustav Mahler, Freud, Karl Kraus, and Einstein, has proved to be the truly positive spirit, Zionism sprang from despair at achieving success along that line. Theodor Herzl not only knew Russian, Austrian, and German anti-Semitism; he also experienced at first hand the campaign of hatred which the Dreyfus trial unleashed in France. He had grown up in a Jewish circle that was no less assimilated than that of any highly educated Jew. But he finally lost faith in the prospects of pluralism amid a world that was rapidly becoming nationalistic and militaristic. His forebodings seem justified today, as I have already indicated. As technology develops, as populations increase, as individual peoples are ceaselessly transformed into rigidly organized power blocs which are engaged in merciless competition and formed into friendly alliances or hostile groups, there is little prospect that European civilization as the nineteenth century knew it will survive in the latter part of the twentieth. Anti-Semitism may have religious origins but it is no longer essentially a religious phenomenon; it is rather a means of manipulation in an age when every economic weakness can be a weak point open to attack by any foreign nationalism that happens to be more vigorously and thoroughly organized. The striking power of the military depends ever more fully on that of the population as a whole, and anti-Semitism is a means of assuring the latter. In the states which had accepted Jews, the Jews used to be for the most part very good and especially patriotic citizens. But if they wanted to survive, they needed, in Herzl's view, an assimilation which went counter to the usual kind: an assimilation not to the state in which they lived but to "the ways of the nations" [2] in general. That is, they needed a territory and an appropriate patriotism of their own. Herzl's book, *The Jewish State,* which marks the beginning of the Zionist movement, expresses his doubt that the European states could take the idea of pluralism seriously in the long run, his doubt that they could leave the individual free, within the community, to follow his own principles. The Zionist movement, with its refusal to trust any longer in the prospects of pluralism or of the civilization of the autonomous individual in Europe, is the radical yet resigned reaction of Judaism to the possibilities thrown open in the last century. The saddest aspect of contemporary history, saddest for the Jews as well as for Europe, is that Zionism has proved a true prophet.

When I said earlier that repressed feelings easily turn against those who resemble the possessor of the feelings, I would not have followed Freud to such an extent, had I not seen such resemblance often given as the reason for irrational hatred. Resemblances do exist between Germans and Jews, as men of insight and the persecutors themselves have acknowledged. "The Germans, like the Jews, will let themselves be oppressed, but they will not let themselves be exterminated any more than the Jews will; they will not be discouraged but will maintain a strong cohesiveness even if they be deprived of their fatherland." [3] The insane dictator who made extermination his program and carried it out as far as he could within the area under his control, said in expressing his more personal thoughts: "Has it not struck you how the Jew is the exact opposite of the German in every single respect, and yet is as closely akin to him as a blood brother?" [4] The points of comparison are clear enough. The Germans became free citizens at a later date than other Western peoples; only at a late date did they create a centralized political state and a position of equality in modern Europe. (*The Belated Nation* is the title of one of Helmuth Plessner's books.[5]) Once admitted on terms of equality to competition with other countries, the Germans won a high place through mercantile proficiency and scientific brilliance, such as were attributed to no other people except the Jews. The complaints of English industrialists at the turn of the century who wanted to stick with habitual methods of production and therefore fell behind their German competitors, read at times like letters written by Germans about the acquisitiveness and unfair methods of the Jews!

Moreover, anyone familiar with America knows the German capacity for assimilation. German immigrants there were known for this quality long before the rise of the modern German empire. Only with difficulty can a Frenchman, or even an Englishman, substitute another tradition for his own, but I myself know Germans, Jewish and non-Jewish alike, who in a short time learn to speak German with an American accent; I could give you the names of colleagues, students, and secretaries. The diligence shown in achieving such an identification betrays both talent and weakness. Yet it was not to such analogies between German and Jew that I wished primarily to draw your attention (for they could be found in many peoples), but to something deeper. Precisely because the Germans reached statehood at such a late date, it was only later than others that they could apply their energies to modern economics, politics, and extension of power. At a time when France was entering upon its Revolution and passing by way of military rule and reaction to it to enrichment for all its citizens, thought was having its heyday in the German lands, where absolutism still held sway. The saying about the nation of poets and thinkers refers to this historical period in which the major German philosophy saw the light of day. The philosophy of other European peoples, especially the English and the French, tended toward nominalism and positivism, for their thinking was directed to the shaping of the real world about them, and in this kind of philosophy the concept serves primarily as a means of achieving empirical goals. In Germany, on the contrary, philosophers have sought to rescue the "idea" in the plenary sense of the word, that is, the "spirit" (*Geist*). Empirical science is to keep its proper field of activity, but the latter is to serve in the realization of a more than empirical reality. In a development which for power and temporal extension can only be compared to the upsurge of some of the arts and intellectual disciplines in Antiquity and the Renaissance, the Kantian theory of the autonomous subject was elaborated into an explicit presentation of the progressive awareness of freedom as the motive force behind world history.

The close relation of idealism to the thinking of the emancipated Jews is confirmed by the great Jewish disciples and followers of the philosophers. It may be seen in particular doctrines of idealism as well as in its overarching structure which combines a sense of reality with an imperturbable attachment to the idea (which is the opposite of reality). Among the particular traits to be found both in idealism and emancipated Jewish thought, I can mention here only one essential one: the impossibility of giving a name to the Divine. According to Hegel the answer to the question of the Unconditioned is to be found in the development of concepts, in which the thinker cannot stop at any single concept as being *the* truth. Everyone knows the story of the disillusionment of Hegel's audiences at Berlin. They came expecting to be given the key to the mystery and the experience of the "Absolute." The professor began with logic and advanced to natural philosophy; in succeeding semesters he dealt with man and his psychology, law, and the state. He showed how history moved from the Asiatic empires via slavery to the Christian nations; he explained the dialectic at work in the development of art and religion to their highest forms. Finally he gave the history of philosophy. Apropos of each philosophical work he sought to show the truth it contained and how the lack or limitations of such truth gave rise to the impulse to go further. Since the presentation of Hegel's own philosophy was to follow, his hearers thought that now at last they would hear the words for the sake of which they had attended the whole long series of lectures. But instead Hegel began all over again with logic!

The story sounds like one from the Talmud, and the similarity is more than accidental. In both cases the issue is a truth which cannot be isolated and positively stated, but which is there nonetheless. This element of contradiction is inherent in the Jewish tradition as it is in dialectical philosophy where it becomes explicit as a moment in the process of thought as it strives toward the truth. That the Jews should through long centuries cling to a doctrine in which neither the reward of individual blessedness nor the eternal punishment of the individual played any key role; that they should remain faithful to a law after the disappearance of the state that might have enforced the law, solely because of the hope in store for the just men of all nations—that is the contradiction which links the Jews with Germany's major philosophy and indeed with all that is popularly or ironically called idealism.

The role played in all this by the concept of the people is highly complex, and I dare not venture into it. I would only like to speak briefly of the analogy between the Jewish and German mentalities as well as the radical difference between them. The Jewish martyrs who over a long period (for example, the Renaissance and Counter-Reform) could like the early Christians have escaped an agonizing death by accepting another faith, had hardly anything to fall back on but the Law which was the cohesive factor in Jewry. Right from the beginning of the modern German empire there developed an idea of mission which, consciously or unconsciously, found its model in the Old Testament. Wilhelm II, to whom (despite justified doubts of his astuteness) the prophetic words about the Yellow Peril are attributed, held the view that Germany was to bring salvation to the world. And I know from personal experience that very many Germans, Jews among them, felt the same way. The dictator whose plans for conquest reproduced Wilhelm's dream, though in a gruesomely distorted way, regarded the Germans as God's people. In the conversation already mentioned, when he was expressing his more personal ideas and when in his convulsive excitement "words failed him," one sentence runs: "There cannot be two Chosen People. We are God's People. Does not that fully answer the question?" [6] Nor was it simply the masses who echoed the mad dream.

The divinization of the nation was due to the fact that the nation was still problematic in its own eyes. Ever since the Empire was founded, German history has been marked by a felt need to enlarge German power in the midst of the older nations, by the struggle for a place in the sun against the Western peoples, and by an ambivalent relation to the Eastern threat. Advocate and critic alike have voiced this outlook. Immediately after enumerating the "many blessings and evils" which Europe owes the Jews,[7] Nietzsche says that there are nations which suffer from, and even want to suffer from, national nerve-fever and political ambition. He offers "today's Germans" as an example [8] and sees anti-Semitism as one consequence of the illness. German energy reminds us in fact of many a campaign in the Bible, for example in the Book of Joshua. But if the political ambition is comparable to the ambition of which the Bible speaks, time has introduced a difference. Between Biblical patriotism and the conduct of those Jews who gave their lives with no thought of eternity, there lies the loss of the promised land; and the latter has not been replaced by a kingdom not of this world. The Jewish lawbreaker of the late Middle Ages, who refused to buy an easier death or even his freedom by conversion, was faithful to something powerless. The concept of God and people merged with the desire to be remembered by the people. The Jew knew of no other reward.

An understanding of the Jews in today's Germany is both difficult and easy. It is difficult for many reasons, including the fact that Germany's collective pride has been more deeply wounded than most people suspect. Franz Wedekind was enthusiastic when the First World War began; he wrote in September, 1914: "If the heroic struggle of the young German Empire is crowned with victory, the sons of Germany will be filled with pride in their country; the obvious justification for that pride, as well as its moral dignity, will raise it far above shrill jingoism and narrow-spirited traditional enmities." [9] He said nothing, however, about what must happen to this pride after the first and second great defeats. Injured pride means a wound in the collectivity no less than in the individual. The Jews who were victims of that pride are now linked in men's minds with the catastrophe and with the violence practiced both by the Germans and on the Germans. In the unconscious, roles are reversed: "It is not the murderer but the victim who is guilty." It is extremely difficult to cure the illness of narcissism; even the generation that was not involved in the catastrophe suffers from a wound it does not know exists. Moreover, the play of political and psychological forces which caused the national nerve-fever has become further complicated in unhealthy ways. When the Third Reich practiced terror on those who were different, it simultaneously did something to the Germans themselves which goes as deep as the external division. To bring this up into awareness and to exorcize it requires a moral process which cannot keep pace with the triumphant growth of the economy. Yet the understanding of the Jews, of which we are speaking, depends on a spiritual change and the disappearance of the trauma.

In addition to this specifically German difficulty there is a more general one: those who hate the Jews, like all who are used to judging the individual in the light of negative aspects of the alien group to which he belongs, judge according to clichés. They are surrounded by a wall of inflexible concepts. Once the wall is built, it takes almost a miracle to break through it. At one time any old woman with a birthmark was a witch; still earlier, any slave was only a thing. Anyone who judges in this fashion is usually not prepared to question his own thinking; he can rationalize his negative outlook but not overcome it. The attempt to convert an anti-Semite is to some extent a contradiction in terms, and any undertaking aimed at creating mutual understanding today must bear this in mind. If we prescind from those who are already won over and only need encouragement, such an undertaking supposes that it is dealing with undecided people who are radically serious about finding the truth.

Young people, we may hope, still have some time to develop a sense whereby they can perceive and affirm the identity that links every man amid the differences that have developed between themselves and others. It is to this end that the struggle against prejudice must be directed. It is true enough that the young know but little about even the recent past, for at present the capacity for remembering is on the wane. National Socialism seems so distant to them that in many countries they hardly know even the name any more. What happened yesterday is over and done with not only for the youth of Germany but for the youth of America or Sweden or even Israel. Historical closeness in time is no more of a guarantee against blindness and oppression than geographical nearness used to be. I do not believe, therefore, that the filling in of gaps in historical knowledge, especially if the new knowledge is a cause for shame, is the best way today of creating the frame of mind which a free society needs. Historical knowledge is important. Even more important, however, is a sensitivity to the forces and methods that made the evil possible. Yet even this is not enough; the younger generation must be educated so that it is critical in the face of demagogy, learns to recognize how demagogy functions in times of economic and political crisis, and possesses the categories with which to distinguish demagogy from a truly rational politics. The decisive thing, in my opinion, is to awaken the interest that finds its happiness in insight into things and men, the kind of insight no longer possible to the consciousness which has ceased to develop. Anyone who has with full awareness found truth in the work of a Jewish poet or a Jewish composer will hardly be inclined to anti-Semitism. Anyone who has taken a serious interest in Jewish culture will easily see through the nonsense peddled by the propagandists of hatred. The decisive point—and the real task of education without which neither the Jewish nor the Christian nor the German cause is helped—is that men should become sensitive not to injustice against the Jews but to injustice as such, not to persecution of the Jews but to any and all persecution, and that something in them should rebel when any individual is not treated as a rational being.

THE ARREST OF EICHMANN
(1960)

A subordinate in the ranks of National Socialism, Eichmann by name, who was specially charged with the
elimination of the Jews in Germany and in German-
occupied countries, has been arrested in Argentina by
Israeli nationals and brought to Israel. There he is to be
tried and judged. The number of Jews murdered at
Eichmann's orders is variously estimated at from three
quarters of a million to four or five million. He was proud
of his role in the "final solution" and, indeed, was on the
side of the law according to the prevailing unjust law. If
the Israeli court wants to prove itself competent, it will
declare itself incompetent.

It is evident that the formal grounds given for the
proceedings are untenable. Eichmann did not commit his
murders in Israel, and Israel cannot want the arrest of
criminals inside the sanctuary which they have, rightly or
wrongly, obtained, to become the rule. Punishment is the
means by which a state forces men to observe the law
within its own boundaries; its purpose is deterrence. All
other theories of punishment are just bad metaphysics. To
suppose, however, that punishment inflicted in Israel will

deter possible imitators of Eichmann is nonsense. Indeed, whatever be the sentence passed on Eichmann in
Israel, it will prove the weakness, not the strength, of
Jews' awareness of their rights; it will be a usurpation, not
a legitimate manifestation, of civil authority. Everyone
knows, moreover, that it is only because of the present
political situation that people are letting pass this kind of
arrest in a foreign country; the procedure itself recalls the
methods used in states quite different from Israel.

The internal grounds given for the arrest and trial are
no less inadequate. The trial, it is claimed, will make the
youth of Israel and other nations aware of the true nature
of the Third Reich. If, however, such knowledge must win
the place it ought to have in the consciousness of present
and future generations, not by way of the solid literature
that is now available in scientific as well as in generally
accessible form in all the major languages, but only by
way of up-to-the-minute trial reports and international
sensationalist journalism, then prospects for that knowledge are poor indeed. The mind upon which the death
of the Jews under Hitler can make an impression only
through new headlines has very little depth and is hardly
likely to retain any recollection of what it reads. It is
difficult to foresee the real effects of repeated references
during a trial to the elimination of the Jews; it is difficult,
that is, to foresee the real political and psychological
effect on various peoples. The youth of Israel and many
people in other countries whom the authorities hope to
win over will entertain the frustrating suspicion that the
dead are here being used as a political or even a pedagogi-
cal tool, a tactical weapon or a piece of propaganda, even
if in the pursuit of a very praiseworthy national purpose.
The opposition of the forces of good to those of destruction around the world will be paralyzed, because here

the opposition is using the very intellectual weapons which the enemy takes for granted. Criminal trials for calculated ends belong in the arsenal of antisemitism, not in that of Judaism. Such trials will certainly not stop the many evil men among the nations of the earth from such crimes as can occur without the earth opening up to swallow the perpetrators.

The expectations of the Israeli authorities concerning the influence of the Eichmann revelations are incorrect. Persecution and mass murder are basic themes of world history. Seldom have they frightened off future Führers and their camp followers. Political systems that use terrorism often become repugnant for a time when they have been defeated by domestic or foreign enemies, but the abhorrence passes and enthusiasm for terrorist methods is kindled anew. For decades after Waterloo no one dared defend Napoleon, to say nothing of the great Revolution. But when Louis Philippe's economic miracle came to pass, Napoleon's casket was brought to Paris and the infamous man finally mounted the new imperial throne, until the Prussians defeated him a second time. Yet at the end of the century France was regarded as the protectress of freedom. The power of forgetfulness is great; it has grown and is still growing with the spread of communications. One novelty drives another from the limelight of press and radio, but the old continues to exert its influence in hidden and uncontrolled ways.

As a final (or foremost) reason for the trial, we hear reparation mentioned as though it were an obvious human necessity. I have a deep distrust of the term reparation. It seems to me to arise in an alien world and to conceal sinister impulses; it reminds me of the Middle Ages and the Inquisition. The very idea that Eichmann could "atone" for his deeds according to a human standard and the sentence of a human judge is a mockery of the sacrifice the Jews made, a gruesome and grotesque mockery. I can much more readily understand the open determination to seek revenge, however poor that revenge would be in comparison with the crimes being avenged. If someone who had lost father and mother because of Hitler's order had ambushed the scoundrel in Argentina and killed him in the street, he would not be acting as a tactician or a pedagogue but as a human being with whom anyone could sympathize. But the trial in Israel, however carefully prepared, in fact precisely because it is being so carefully staged, offends right feeling.

The desire to prevent Eichmann from taking part in the plans of the more recent agents of fascism is understandable, but the desire to punish him for his criminal deeds is beneath Israel's dignity. No people has suffered more than the Jews from that kind of mentality. The refusal to accept violence as a proof of the truth is a perennial trait in Jewish history, and Judaism has turned the suffering it endured in consequence of this refusal into a factor in its own unity and permanence. Instead of either leading to redemption or giving rise to some special malice or vileness (traits not lacking, after all, in Jews any more than in other peoples), injustice has in their case become a mode of experience. Suffering and hope have become inseparable in Judaism. At one point in their history the European peoples became aware of this connection and, in their confession of the martyred redeemer, introduced into the godhead itself the torments which Jews were willing to suffer for the sake of that ultimate future they could not abandon. The acceptance of destiny became a religion. Jews, however, are not ascetical people, as the first Christians were; they have never glorified or worshipped or sought or praised suffering but only experienced it. Yet more than for other peoples suffering is inextricably intertwined with their memory of the dead. According to the Jewish law men cannot become saints through suffering, as in Christianity; suffering simply colors remembrance of the dead with an infinite tenderness that does not depend on the consoling thought of eternal life. The Jew in whom the sight of the imprisoned Eichmann arouses a desire to see him suffer has not reflected seriously enough on his own existence. "An eye for an eye," says a legal principle in the Bible. But even if imagination were not forced to admit its inadequacy in attempting to apply the principle to Eichmann, history has provided religion with instructive experience: to undertake an unnecessary punishment of Eichmann amounts to treating him in the way that earns the Jewish dead the love of their people.

The Israeli politicians who must guide the new state in a rapidly changing world are too caught up in activity to dwell on the thoughts we have been suggesting. The philosopher is not a practical man. He argues the incompetence of the court and asks that Eichmann be returned to the country from which he was spirited away. The philosopher believes that no good can come of the trial, either for the security or the situation of the Jew in the contemporary world, or even for Jewish self-awareness. The trial is a repetition: Eichmann will cause harm a second time.

FEUDAL LORD, CUSTOMER,
AND SPECIALIST

The End of the Fairy Tale of the Customer as King
(1964)

Now that the bourgeois world is entering a new situation which may be interpreted either as more rational or as regressive, the forms of human relationship which originated in the feudal order and were transposed to a new level in the bourgeois order are about to be liquidated. Bourgeois culture was deeply influenced by the dignity, honor, and freedom of the feudal lord and, in the last analysis, of the absolute ruler; it transferred these attributes to every individual man and especially to anyone who was well-off. Works of art, language, personal culture, forms of intercourse in business and private life, all took over the symbols of that bygone social distinction which they were rejecting. It has always been characteristic of liberal civilization that hierarchy and subordination are its freely adopted form. Yet, the more unquestioningly and profoundly the demonstrations of honor proper to feudal times continued to be adapted, even if in fragmentary form, and practiced by the bourgeois strata of society, the more widespread did interior independence become, and the more remote any lording it over others as well as any barbarism.

Classical bourgeois England, Voltaire the deadly foe of repressive systems, Goethe son of a Frankfurt bourgeois family, all wanted to give unqualified respect to the nobility. Businessmen accepted the same situation, but transposed to a different sphere. The ideal place for observing bourgeois manners is the market place. In the labor market indeed, especially at the beginning, it was a matter of weakness encountering power rather than citizen encountering citizen. Moreover, since the market (that is, the selling and buying of material goods) depended in other areas too on the labor market, it manifested only very poorly the relations between free men. In addition, elegant shops were less open than they are today to the buyer of modest means. But where such a person did buy, he was served, and the reference to a bygone servant-relationship which the very word "service" implies was not without influence on the manner in which the simple act of buying and selling was performed.

Once the Ancien Régime had collapsed, the manners and ways of thought of its former representatives took on new life. The desire for nobility, which Molière caricatures in *The Bourgeois Gentleman,* became productive in the new atmosphere. As late as the end of the last century the "highly esteemed" recipient of a commercial offer could be sure of the "humble and obedient respect" of the offerer, not simply in the latter's epistolary style but in his whole bearing. The principle of exchange which has always regulated the peacable relations of equals and which became a principle of civilization once formal equality became widely accepted was not in any way affected by this development, for traditional concepts and feelings were adapted to fit the new life-style. As the idea of being a "purveyor to the king" motivated the choice of profession among bourgeois youth and pointed the way for them to go, so their dealings with prospective customers (and who did not fall into that category?) and especially with anyone who had already presented himself as a buyer, were marked by courteous attention. The principle which every employer tried to drum into salesmen and salesgirls—"The customer is always right"—derives in substance from the time of the absolute ruler. For economic reasons the old motifs continued to control the way men were formed. To the extent that mercantile activity contributed to the model of a proper life, respect for the customer became, consciously or unconsciously, an element of education. The child did not have to wait until he was in school or until he grew up and was working; even in his early contacts with his parents he was being shaped in accordance with the requirements he would have to meet as an adult. Along with sensitivity to others and their wishes he was developing the impulse to satisfy these wishes.

The readiness to see in the other a potential buyer, the inclination to serve and please, were habitual throughout wide strata of society. Along with ruthlessness in one's own business and in commercial competition, there went an adaptability (whether the divergent traits were found in the same individuals or distributed among distinct agents in the economy). There was no pity for the weak; the competitor was to be fought and the employee exploited. But the customer was to be wooed and flattered. All this was typical of society as a whole. The act of buying and selling in a shop that dealt in only one article was a modest symbol of business dealings in the larger world. Neither friendliness nor expert knowledge, not even a favorable ratio between price and value, were enough to produce the all-important result. The business man who traveled to meet a business friend abroad or welcomed him at his own place of business or in his own home, had to have good manners and a familiarity with other languages, countries, and ways. Anything that could pave the way to contacts with potential buyers and win their good will fell within the businessman's purview. Bourgeois culture, like any other, had its foundation in specific interests, even if it were not reducible to the latter. In the art of selling the sensibilities of the customer were of course taken into account. However soberly and critically the customer might examine the goods offered him, the behavior of the seller was not without influence in the transaction. According to circumstances that behavior was more than window-dressing. Even the man in the street experienced in the act of buying a little of his own freedom and of respect for himself as subject.

The change which is now going on in the buyer's position—a change which is determinative for the social life of the individual and for his self-awareness—cannot but affect the human makeup as it is inevitably caught up into the economic and technological development with its dizzying rate of acceleration. The rising living standard and the improved condition of large sectors of the population which at an earlier time were not part of the bourgeoisie are effecting a revolution in the mechanisms of buying and selling, even among the upper bourgeoisie. Even in the area of daily shopping a transformation is taking place which is more far-reaching than the drastic change from the specialized store to the department store which Emile Zola depicted in his novel *Le paradis des dames*. In the process of selling household necessities and especially food, those who help in the selling have a few necessary tasks but otherwise are only stopgaps, temporary substitutes for self-service and automated equipment. This is true of the economy generally for that part of the work force which does not simply supervise auto-mation. As formerly, so now the customer is a subject, but he is now to some extent a self-supporting subject: he must quickly orient himself, know his way around among the current standardized brands, and react promptly as though he were working in a factory. In modern stores which are organized with psychological expertise, stores that are for the most part chain-stores in which price and quality are determined somewhere far from the place of the transaction and are minimally subject to bargaining, the resigned gestures of the old-style housewife as she tests the proferred goods may still be justified in excep-tional cases but they are nonetheless an antiquated as she herself is.

Within the same price-range qualitative differences in the products of various companies are small; in most cases a person who runs from store to store is only wasting time and energy, whether he is interested in preserves or automobiles. The closing time, determined by the civil authorities and marked by an almost military uniformity in most countries, forces the less well-off, who have only the regular hours available for making purchases, to make them hastily; so too, for the sake of a regulated free-time, the closing hour limits even further the already modest freedom of the small property-owner. Standardization and the decision by those in power on the goods to be offered are to the advantage of the general public by reducing the need for personal judgment of differences. Attention is focused on statistics, on the overall number of people who use a product. These users are counted and mani-pulated. To the extent that the individual does not dis-appear entirely, he is a marginal figure, a customer in a derogatory sense of the term.

On the whole, the customer, or rather the female customer (for women still take care of most things needed for daily use), may put herself into the hands of the company; in cases of doubt the company has already anticipated her decision by means of questionnaires and statistics. Legal regulations, consumer organizations, even the mass media when they turn their attention to industry, all provide a certain amount of protection for the customer. Not too long ago President Johnson sent the American Congress a message requesting further laws to protect the buyer. According to his message, the idea that the customer must watch out for himself is outdated; among other things, exact labeling and clear, full descriptions of products are needed. Each buyer must be able to see at a glance what is being offered; the label must be a mute salesman. On similar grounds the German government decided to establish an Institute for Product Testing. The personal relationship is being eliminated from the act of buying and selling. There is no longer room for acts of courtesy to individuals, for the old bow to the customer is being replaced by advertising, the latter, which constitutes a special large sector in the division of labor, being professionally standardized and rationalized, no less than the advertised goods or services. The development of advertising is hastening the process of monopolization which it expresses, and is at the same time freeing an important social activity from its dependence on the amiability of any individual seller.

To the extent that deference to the individual, whether in the business sphere or the erotic, is still required, it is inculcated in the home, at school, and in vocational training, but in a calculating, superficial, and utilitarian way: not as a genuinely personal trait of character but simply as the more prudent way to act. Hymns of praise belong in advertisements and on billboards, in the illustrated magazines or on the screen. In dealing with customers and between lovers, on the contrary, the idea is to eliminate all the nonsense and get down to the real business at hand. The complex world here becomes one-dimensional and transparent. Even fanaticism today is but a despairing admission that one can no longer believe in anything. The fact that advertising has kept up with the times and become a special branch of business is both an advance and a setback. It is expertly planned in scientifically outfitted offices and laid out by professional artists and caption-writers; yet the intellectual effort expended on it is aimed at intensifying the effect on potential buyers, not at heightening the level of the product's true worth. Such work is a posthumous justification of the old-time puffer. His methods are still useful in dealing with the present-day general public, both in the market place and in politics. Businesses which still cater to individual customers, for example the custom tailor, nowadays either serve only the rich or else offer goods that not infrequently are inferior to mass-produced ready-made goods.

The sphere in which the buyer is, at least initially, directly dependent on the person of the supplier is that of the specialist. As science and technology have become more differentiated, the specialist's functions have multiplied and are acquiring an ever more decisive role in economics and politics. The relation of the customer to the seller of a specialized service is, abstractly considered, still that of payer and payee, but, from a psychological and social point of view, the relationship is only distantly like that which was once familiar in the market place. The dealings of specialist and client remind us at least as much of feudal lord and citizen as they do of buyer and seller. The conditions of mass society and, most immediately, the decreased intensity of competition in comparison with the liberalist period are causing the roles to be reversed. The buyer must increasingly adapt himself to the supplier, in all matters from the date of the appointment to the way the appointment proceeds.

The change is due to the nature of the situations in question. If the man in the street goes to a lawyer to buy advice, he must explain his case and ask his question; from this point on the lawyer asks the questions, and, the more competent he is, the more penetrating the questions will be. The customer gives answers; as the case requires, he provides evidence. The situation is the same with other experts, to the extent that they are available at all to the private citizen. The architect thinks of the building contractor as a layman who tells him what he needs and what he can pay. The builder must then accept the architect's views when it comes to the suitableness or timeliness of any further wishes the former may express. To the extent that a house need not follow a predetermined plan but can in shape and execution express the builder's personality, "builder" is assumed to mean, not, for example, the future inhabitant, but the architect whom he commissions. This state of affairs has long been accepted by the public, for it flows from a social dynamism too powerful to resist. The act of purchasing no longer fosters bourgeois self-awareness. Instead, the well-grounded authority of the specialist is promoting on a large scale a type of accommodation already known in other areas, namely, a readiness to acknowledge and obey instructions that are not evident to the recipient. The specialist, as purveyor of advanced skills, is radically out of place in a market economy. He rather points, on the one hand, to a bygone day when the priest alone knew how to achieve the goals everyone was striving for, and, on the other, to a future in which an unimaginably complicated social mechanism will operate without friction and the very idea of individual freedom and autonomy will be outdated and meaningless.

The specialist has always mistrusted the very idea of customer. The area of the market in which this mistrust is especially clear today—the waiting rooms and consulting rooms of practicing physicians—has never adopted a commercial terminology. Yet if we compare medicine as practiced in the heroic period down to the turn of the century (a period which paved the way for today's immense skill in healing) with the contemporary medical business, or the old family doctor with the internist whom people must now visit, the radical difference in methods and in range of effectiveness is quite clear.[1]

The more responsible and dedicated the physician, the more distressing his own situation will appear to him. Only those most favored by destiny can temporarily avoid the consequences of that situation. Yet the organizations involved—medical societies and medical schools, along with public opinion—can, quite naturally, see only the other side of the coin. They denounce the obliging doctor who listens to the patient's wishes, the druggist who lets his heart be touched, and even the undisciplined patient who instead of obeying orders insists on his layman's wishes being met. In one of countless articles against the craze for pills we read: "At this point the individual really ceases to be a patient and becomes a customer." Correct. Patients, like individuals generally in our managed society, must adapt themselves; the customer thinks of himself, on the contrary, as someone to be obeyed.

The feudal appearance of the bourgeois world is vanishing; many factors converge here to remove the aureole of magic from developments that have long since been described by the sociologists. At a time when the perfection of observational instruments of every kind is causing language itself to lose its expressive quality and to take on more and more exclusively the character of a set of signs, even the notion of the infinite meaning and value of every individual soul has become outmoded. Religion itself is in the process of adapting to these new circumstances.[2] The customer's loss of his regal status is part of the same process that we see in the resigned attitude of Christianity: the process of being struck dumb amid endless noise. It is clear that the improved material position of wide strata of the population is connected with, and indeed largely conditions, the loss of the individual's illusion that he is a free subject. Yet in today's individual, for all that he is more modest and malleable, bourgeois subjectivity does not disappear, as feudal self-awareness did at an earlier time. The fact is rather that self-awareness in contemporary society is directly connected with belonging to some collectivity: to an age group or vocational group, and ultimately to the nation. The divergence between individual and group that is now disappearing continues to show up among stunted individuals, criminals, and people who can assert themselves only by opposition to everything else.

We see the process of leveling down not least in politics. When in the bourgeois period economically self-sufficient people, who were rather numerous at one time, gave allegiance to one of the parties, the sense of independence they had acquired in other areas made them feel that here too they were customers. They gave priority to one or another enterprise and expected results. Parliamentary delegates were to represent the interests of their constituency's businesses, to promote low or high tariffs, to defend the production of raw materials or finished goods, light or heavy industry, and to see to it that the heads of the various branches of government followed these leads. Like other businesses, the shop of politics was open to the public.

The electioneering trips of candidates in England and America and candidates' personal subservience to the voters still remind us of the liberal type of democracy. In the outer darkness was the proletariat, whether it belonged to a party or not; it was a threatening, non-bourgeois element. Today the workers in many countries are a powerful force, and their leaders vie with others for a share in the social product and, ultimately, in political power. The relation of member to party and delegate to leadership (if we leave the economic giants out of consideration) is one of party discipline. In politics as in the goods market, no one cultivates individuals; psychological and sociological experience allows the manipulation of masses of people. The watchword is brevity and accuracy. The characteristic traits of the past—the special self-awareness in business and politics, and the human qualities connected with that self-awareness—cannot be separated from the economic limitations, the pauperization and injustice of the period to which they belonged. Such traits were a by-product of a state of affairs in which historical progress, industry, and the science and technology that went with it depended on the largest possible number of relatively independent and competing producers, on the one hand, and a hungry proletariat on the other. But the more planned the society, whether in late democratic or totalitarian form, the more removed from reality are bourgeois culture and sensibility.

Devotion to what is now passing away is not simply to be put aside as romantic, just because the infamous whole of which it was a part fell so far short of the norms of justice. A proper state of affairs cannot come into being without memory. What we call Western civilization still thinks it has a spiritual advantage over the rest of the world; the East, of course, challenges this view. But, however much the social situation of the two differs, it seems to be slowly becoming identical. There is now a greater degree of regulation, planning, and management in the West, while in the East the reins seem to be slackening, even if only now and then and very cautiously. In the bourgeois state individual freedom is in process of becoming simply a matter of "free time" rather than developing in a qualitative way.

In any event, the realm of freedom which, according to theorists whom the East invokes, is to be brought into existence only through Communism, and which the West has always, and rightly, contrasted with the regimes current in the East, has antecedents in even the smallest details of bourgeois life. To forget or suppress the memory of those antecedents would be to retrogress. Philology and academic history provide the material and are concerned with what can be documented; moreover, in earlier periods these disciplines dealt with a more neutral area than they do in our own controversial times. To recall today—even in the unscientific fashion in which it has been done here—the former situation of a customer in a shop is to supply one microscopic detail for our efforts in shaping the future. It would take another lecture to discuss practical consequences in regard to education, daily dealings with others, business methods, and the relation of specialist to layman.

THREATS TO FREEDOM
(1965)

My subject today is the threat to freedom. I ask your
indulgence if I so formulate the theme as to avoid any
theological or metaphysical reflections on freedom and
approach the concept in a strictly empirical way. Indeed,
I am encouraged to do so by theology itself. I am thinking here of Catholic and especially of Evangelical utterances on this idea of freedom, for they seem, in one important aspect at least, to be in substantial agreement with
the Enlightenment, Voltaire, and above all, Immanuel
Kant. The speculative mind admittedly feels it necessary
to postulate freedom in a transcendental sense. But within
our spatio-temporal world, inquiring reason must look for
the causes of human actions and regard the latter as no
less conditioned than any other event in the universe. The
doctrines of God's gracious choice [predestination] and
of the intelligible nature of reality are very intimately
related to each other. According to both the Enlightenment and religion empirical human freedom is not something unconditioned but is rather the real possibility of
distinguishing between various actions as between the
numerous ways that may be taken, interiorly and ex-

teriorly, subjectively and objectively, in a given situation. Whether the measure of freedom depends more on psychic or on physical conditions (on the objects that present themselves for choice or on the subject's capacity to make use of them) can be determined for individuals and groups only through analysis of the particular case. The modes of action which in fact lie open to a man, along with his presence of mind and his personal make-up, combine to provide the freedom available at the moment. It is not the characteristic elements in the concept of freedom but rather the kind and range of the motives on which freedom at any moment depends, that open up infinite vistas for us as we tackle the subject of freedom.

As we all know, in the Middle Ages and well into modern times the commands of God and man's fear of damnation played as determining a role in individual practical decisions and in the general orientation of life as did the fear of earthly force; in most instances, indeed, the former and the latter coincided. Even in our own supposedly enlightened age when men seldom set aside social advantage, prestige, and health in order to obey religious impulses, the same anxieties and convictions that formerly played a conscious determining role seem to me to be still at work: a man will want to see a dear friend again in eternity, he will want to pass beyond with a conscience at peace. Theological concepts may have been sublimated and reinterpreted in the light of modern science, but the religious motives which can come into conflict with secular motives have—as far as I can see—continued substantially unchanged in the authentic believer.

I must also ask your indulgence in regard to the critical moment implicit in my theme. Please do not look on me as an enemy of the better. The saying about the sweaty feet of progress comes, after all, from a man who was more loyal to progress than the pragmatists were: from Karl Kraus. When we discuss the contemporary threat to freedom, we cannot avoid highlighting what is negative by comparison with earlier periods and especially with the period just now past, the late nineteenth century. I know of no era in which productive forces, technology, commerce, and the scientific and political situation developed more quickly and in a more wrenching way than in the last hundred years. If, then, the positive aspects of this change—scientific conquests, success in bomb production and space travel, raising of the living standard, the "awakening" of the Asiatic and African peoples—are greeted with skepticism, if the concomitant results which detract from freedom, or the regressions and world-wide major catastrophes that are inseparable from or even provide the conditions for such progress are pointed out in a critical way, and if comparisons are made with the ages before such progress in order to highlight the negative side of the latter, these criticisms often seem reactionary, or sentimental and romantic. But this very objection to such criticism is really an apology for the existing situation.

If social progress is really to live up to its name, it must preserve what was good in the past. To suppress the thought of the cost a culture pays for its new miracles and to adopt an official optimism is to be enslaved to an evil status quo. East and West alike bear witness to this. It is true enough that a critical grasp of the present supposes insight into the injustice and lies of the past, and especially a knowledge of how the earlier culture contradicted its own ideas: how Christian history contradicted Christianity and bourgeois history bourgeois ideals, to say nothing of Communism and Karl Marx. It is also true, however, that critical theory, which we follow, gives unquestioned priority to existing reality as its object. This holds for time as well as space. It is simply proof of a nationalist ideology to live in one's own country (Germany, for example) and spend the time waxing hot about Russia or America, instead of using what ought to be and what could be as the basis for a critical examination of one's own vital situation. The demand that we construct a better social totality and develop in a positive way the new possibilities opened up by technology can be met only when our conscience refuses to rest easy with the disappearing freedom of the individual; the fact that such freedom was earlier limited to the bourgeoisie can make no difference here.

I shall begin with an historical reflection. The very passage of freedom from aristocrat to citizen was in many respects linked to a retrogression of freedom. At the beginning of the nineteenth century, despite the fact that workhouses still existed, the proletarian was no longer, in theory at least, a serf, and others could not behave toward him as they had in an earlier day. The social history of England, after the machine wreckings of the thirties, was, as we know, a struggle against the power of the entrepreneur in favor of democracy. As the freedom of the dependent classes increased, the independent people (the bourgeoisie) found themselves forced, in their dealings with each other and with their employees, to a further development of varied relationships and thus of their own character. The relation to the workers, no less than economic competition, trade, and industry, led to the multiplication and refinement of the ways in which men deal with each other and, consequently, to a greater inner freedom in comparison with the nobility from whom the externals of conduct were derived. The limitation of freedom had caused the further development of freedom. Whether the contemporary technological revolution which makes a better and more secure life possible for the majority in the developed countries also helps them to a greater human differentiation, as the eighteenth-century revolution did for the bourgeoisie, is a question we can only raise here without going into it fully. We shall simply mention briefly some points which suggest a negative answer to the question.

The shaping of thought and feeling through the mass media and other methods of influencing people, the lessening of nuanced personal thinking through the controlled presentation of both the objects of thought and the ways of approaching them, the suggestion and manipulation that are bound up with the active supplying of information—all this has been pointed out too often for us to have to dwell on it here. The stereotyped rejection of television, for example, which was still customary a few years ago in German families which considered themselves educated highlights with special clarity the impossibility of turning the clock back. It may indeed be true that when a child acquires its first knowledge of the world not through interaction with his father but through the screen and its images, not through spontaneous stimuli but through immediate reaction to signs, the end result is intellectual passivity. Yet the absence of a set from his parents' home only leads to the child being looked down on by his companions in school, to feelings of inferiority and worse. The flight into the past is no help to the freedom that is being threatened.

Among the less frequently discussed changes in human relationships is the disappearance of immediacy in personal intercourse. The enormous dynamism of modern society is out of all proportion to the initiative of the individual. For this and other reasons inherent in modern life the individual does not experience the other person as, let us say, some one close to or distant from himself in outlook, someone to be convinced, someone involved with him in his own affairs or to be drawn into such involvement. Commitment to another is only a hindrance to one's career or, as one bright young woman student put it, a label one attaches to oneself which can only do harm if it does not carry with it the promise of outward success. In America, where in many areas of life the point has already been reached toward which Europe is still moving, relatives and older friends who want to be helpful will advise the inexperienced younger person as he goes to a party: "Don't raise controversial questions, don't hold on too hard to any opinion, don't talk too long about any one subject, tell a joke occasionally so people can laugh, don't be too serious." There is even a pamphlet giving the young man rules for how to act with a female acquaintance, when and how to call for her in the evening, how to invite her into his car, and what is involved in "steady dating." If he is thinking of marriage and hesitating between several of his girl friends, he will find a list of the possible traits of her parents and her own character. Check off the positive traits; the girl who scores the most points is the best risk. The choice will then be a rational one and have the greatest chance of success; it will certainly be no worse than a choice which has been made in a moment of passion but nonetheless binds the man for his whole future. Don't think of this pamphlet as an isolated phenomenon or as the work of an author or publisher bent on sensationalism. It is rather a symbol of maturity and of the regulation of which society today stands everywhere in need. And it is published by the Y.M.C.A., the largest organization of its kind in the world.

The regulation of relations between individuals does not come solely from conscious guidance. The thin walls of modern skyscrapers can here be taken as symbolic. One's neighbor listens in on one's conversation; even the telephone is not securely private; one is wise to say only what one is willing to have everyone know. Aldous Huxley, George Orwell, and Vance Packard have made us aware of how progress is accompanied by the spread of the instruments and methods of spying. The influence of all this on our speech is evident. The sentence, the judgment, and ultimately the thought are formed so as at least not to hinder success. In the older generation caution is still exercised by conscious processes: a person must be on his best behavior. Among the young, however, speech is experienced as already affected by publicity. Apart from secrets, everyone thinks and speaks in the way proper to his group or profession.

One effect of this development is that the great words, even the religious and national words, including freedom, lose their meaning. They function as elements of convention rather than of conscience. The more they become everyday currency, the less they are taken seriously. A while back I received a well-meaning pamphlet on educational reform, with the request that I go through it very carefully. On the first page the word freedom was used thirteen times. In my answer I said that if I should find the word honesty used thirteen times in a business advertisement, I would surely buy nothing from such a store. The great words become clichés, and language a means of causing no offense in a world that has something to offer me. The decay of individual expressiveness, which is effected in home and school through the schematization of language, is carried further in professional life. The cultivation found in the bourgeois home, which was staffed by servants, and the forms of personal behavior to the business friend, which in the nineteenth century still had economic significance, have long since become things of the past due to a far more developed division of labor in business and to other mechanical devices. When the great corporations initiate and develop business relationships, they do not allow themselves to be influenced in the slightest by the refined attitudes and cultivated speech of the directors of other organizations. In trying to come to grips with the complicated structure of reality (we say nothing here of technological and political capabilities), the whole point is to act with self-awareness and in a positive way, to set oneself off from others as little as possible, and to use speech simply as a means of communication; a specialized kind of self-expression only creates barriers and induces doubts in others.

As the demands made on men in an increasingly automated world become less differentiated, so do impulses and characters. In Rousseau's *Emile* or Goethe's *Wilhelm Meister* the education of an individual is regarded as a very unique and unrepeatable process. At the present time, on the contrary, education too is becoming schematized. Even the desire for freedom and individual treatment, which in many respects must be surrendered because the schools and universities are overcrowded, begets its contrary: a multiplication of machines and a consequent depersonalization. In the school the teachers are overburdened by the range of material and the number of students, and must make use of teaching aids already common in other contexts: the recording and the didactic film, if they are to provide their charges with that preparation for life which they rightly expect from the school. In similar fashion, academic difficulties at the university level cannot be overcome without further technical help. The struggle for a place in the huge auditoriums, the lectures, and the endless examinations by the professor who is himself plagued by a ceaselessly growing body of professional literature and the endless conferences required of him, inexorably necessitate some form of relief: recorded and broadcast lectures, increased use of machines, detailed regulations. The number not only of professorial chairs but of other academic positions as well is out of all proportion to the need. If the freedom of choice of future clientele is to be broadened or, rather, re-created, there is no alternative but to steer such students into the more promising disciplines, to regulate study in a more extensive way, to concentrate attention more and more on the discipline once chosen and on those secondary disciplines that contribute to it, to allow no more digressions into other areas of study, to limit the number of semesters a student may attend, and to pay even less attention than now to general education.

It is evident that the limitation of freedom for the sake of freedom has always been necessary and is even inseparable from the very idea of freedom. But the principle has not always worked out in the same way in each historical period. In a given historical situation regulation, however clearly reasonable, can turn into an obstacle and be a symptom of regression. Please allow me here a philosophical digression, a kind of confession not required by my subject or by considerations arising from any of the contemporary disciplines of which we have been speaking. The individual man may be bent on freedom and redemption. Mankind as a whole, however, is unique in that it has always asserted itself, and still does so today, through domination, exploitation, slaughter, and oppression of other creatures or even, if need be, of the human race itself. Nothing, not even truth and religion, has been too sacred to be turned into a tool of power. Idealistic philosophy has chosen to maintain that limitations introduced for the sake of greater freedom must indeed lead men into the realm of freedom. Materialist philosophy has accepted the same view while applying it differently. It is true enough, of course, that social freedom is never achieved without force. Numerous unsavory activities are required if society is to be held together, including the maintenance of prisons and the production of murderous weapons. To do away with these would be to give up life itself. But reflection on the really operative conditions of existence ought to prevent the historically minded person from indulging in optimism about the future. In 1910, people who were aware of themselves as Germans said, when the question of war came up: "There will be no more war; the Kaiser will not allow it." What in fact occurred was a retrogression to a stage much earlier than that of the previous century. The breakthroughs and very great inventions we now have are intimately connected with the terrible events we have ourselves experienced.

But let us return to the academic professions and the part they play in the relationships between men. The university produces the specialist. As the range of knowledge increases, so does specialization and the inevitable reification of interpersonal relations. Back at the turn of the century it was still possible for a keen student to acquire a grasp not only of the whole field of which his professional concentration was part, but of neighboring fields as well, and even of one or another discipline in other academic areas. Today it is still customary to devote the first few semesters, partly as taste suggests, partly as the entrance examinations require, to the acquisition of knowledge in a number of areas. But as the course of studies progresses, and especially during the period of practical education that follows, there is an increasing specialization. For conquests in particular fields bring ever more numerous subdivisions into existence, and the mastery of any one of these requires as much exact knowledge as had previously been required by the whole of a particular science or even by the whole of that once all-embracing philosophy which has now been downgraded to the rank of a specialized discipline. At the same time, the character of knowledge is changing. The chemist of an earlier day was not limited to a merely theoretical understanding of the nature and use of various chemicals. Today, however, the marvelous knowledge communicated at the university, however much it may embrace the whole of chemistry, remains theoretical and general in relation to the highly differentiated technologies used in industry. The student of chemistry, more than the student of other sciences, must occupy himself through endless semesters with an astonishing number of subordinate specializations. Yet when he finally begins work in an industry as a young Ph.D., he must in many respects start all over again. Academic specialization is inadequate; it must be carried further when practical application is begun.

In few fields are the effects of such scientific progress on the relation between men and their free intercourse so evident as in medicine. Everyone admits that insight into the functioning and pathology of man's organs has been extraordinarily increased. The few illnesses which still resist modern science are being so carefully studied that doubt about the final outcome is hardly possible any longer. Indeed, if society could devote to medical research even a part of the sums that have to be spent on defense and related matters, cancer and numerous other diseases that still endanger us today would very probably have long since been conquered. Furthermore, an ever increasing specialization in medicine has long been taken for granted, for it is closely connected with the increased possibilities of providing medical assistance. It is inevitable that research and treatment should be divided up among a growing number of categories of doctors, that the competence of the practicing physician should become ever more limited in comparison with the range of scientific knowledge, and that the communication of specialists both among themselves and with sick people at home and in hospitals should become increasingly formal and complicated. For many reasons, the doctor's familiarity with the individual case has become a thing of the past, for of its nature such familiarity always has a historical dimension. By this I mean that it does not depend simply on the information given in a case history but requires a grasp of various biographical, familial, and characteriological contexts; it was the kind of knowledge a family doctor used to have of his bourgeois patients. Along with the specialization which has radically changed the relationship of doctor and patient, the method of treatment has also changed. Personal examination of the patient has largely given way, at least in the major cities, to examination with the aid of machines. It has become unusual for a doctor to listen directly to a patient's heart instead of taking an electrocardiogram; at best such direct auscultation is only supplementary. Even the doctor's practice of at least himself examining electrocardiograms is outdated in principle. We now have machines that can make more accurate evaluations of them than the general physician can, even if the latter did not already have far too little time for it. The machine observes microscopic differences which escape man's diagnostic powers; in the most up-to-date institutions the machine even catches nuances which escape the unaided eye, and symptoms to which the overworked diagnostician cannot possibly attend. Responsible medical men have therefore come to rely more and more on machines for examination and diagnosis. In private practice and especially in hospitals, the more seriously a doctor takes his role, the more this role comes to resemble that of a manager in industry. The relation to the object—in this instance, the sick person, the patient—has come to be so mediated by machines and their operating personnel that we can no longer speak of any free, mutual, spontaneous interaction between doctor and client. Such at least is the trend. The customer, as in every monopoly, is confronted with a class of professionals. The more patient and obedient to directions he is, the better his prospect that the gigantic system, this marvel of technology, will produce health for him, as other manufacturers produce automobiles for the unskilled buyer. The more advanced the science and technology, the less need the consumer expect to exercise any greater freedom in the transaction than is involved in stating his need, obeying directions, and paying his bill.

Diminutions of freedom in human relationships are thus the price to be paid for the greater measure of freedom that derives from a general rise in the living standard and a longer life-expectancy. Among these diminutions is the automatic reaction to the directives of experts, a reaction which is a typical and symptomatic response not only to the doctor but to the specialist or other authority in general. In the age of liberalism freedom was closely bound up with mercantile and other productive enterprises. In the so-called social market-economy the same role is played by obedience at the practical level to those who know better: from the professionals in politics, industry, government, and unions to the traffic policeman. The superiority and majesty of the customer, which is still an important factor in foreign policy between nations, plays hardly any role now when the individual is faced with the technology of advertising, the standardization of merchandise, and other economic realities. Even the "free time" (leisure), with which freedom is at times confused, in the form, for example, of a long trip, is usually organized by experts.

Freedom, however, is a matter not only of holidays but of other hours not occupied by professional work or household duties: the evening at home with the family, Sundays, church-going. To what extent have religion and family been affected by developments so dangerous to the civilization we still call Christian? Can it not be said that religion means interior independence of this world, or freedom, even in the empirical sense? Think, for example, of the Gospel of St. John. Has not Christianity, at least in many Protestant interpretations of it, represented opposition to the authority vested in the heathen powers? Do not the account of God creating sun and moon, and the doctrine of his omnipotence mean that contrary to every form of paganism, no power and no being, neither man nor gods, are to rule my life in depth but only God's will and word? And that we, for our part, cannot through any rite or institution or worldly covenant, or even through asceticism, influence Him to whom we are responsible? Does not Christianity, thus understood, stand in utter opposition to conformism, however much secular authority may often have been indebted to religion in this respect? Non-conformity, freedom, self-determined obedience to Someone Other than the status quo may be regarded as typically Christian realities. The important question, however, is: In what sense, on what grounds, in what direction is man to seek to resist this world for the sake of God? To what security is the man who trusts in God to cling as he makes his decision? The answer might be: To the commandment of brotherly love. I do not presume to try to make this latter more concrete. I would simply like to indicate what, in the light of personal experience, it means to me, and why I believe that even this highest of freedoms is not exempt from the threats which history brings with it.

In Judaism and Christianity love of neighbor has always played an essential role as norm of right action. In Judaism, the religion I myself profess, such love was far less connected than in Christianity with the idea of the individual soul and a life after death. Expectation centered rather on the Messiah who would appear on earth some day and lead the just men of every nation to Zion. This belief was constantly reinvigorated by the experience of earthly injustice; it determined both the orthodox Jew's scrupulous observance of all rites and the liberal Jew's adherence to his religion. The expectation that against all probability and despite the previous course of history paradise would some day come, as the Torah and the prophets had promised, was the source of solidarity among Jews and between Jews and outsiders who were upright men. In the eyes of the Jewish mother shone the realization that long after her death her son might experience Messiah's coming or even himself be Messiah. The love of the Christian mother was—in all humility but no less assurance—sustained by the belief that her child belonged to the elect and had an immortal soul. The heightening and ennobling of natural maternal affection by religion has at times affected the lives of those who were loved and cherished in this way as children. Psychological research tells us that the first months and years of a person's life exercise a decisive influence on his later character.[1] They frequently determine whether the person will have a capacity for genuine love or be at bottom cold and self-centered so that everyone who has to deal with him will be simply a means, never an end. What empirical freedom means in the person who has been religiously educated (in the good sense) in comparison with the freedom of the person never touched by such training, is the capacity for dedication and for acting according to the model provided by the founder of Christianity; we see it concretely in those who have been martyrs of goodness. At bottom it is the same thing that we find in secularized form in the French Revolution, the American Constitution, and the teaching of Marx; the thing that finally loses its meaning when it is appropriated by the individual only in a purely conceptual way and not through personal experience. If a loving mother, or some woman who replaces her, really helps a child at the beginning, then Christianity can become a reality in his life. Mary's role in great religious art, therefore, has a positive value and significance. But social change has affected the relations of parent and child, and the motive of love of neighbor, which in large measure determined behavior other than conformity to the world, has itself been drawn into the current of change. It is evident, after all, that even love between the sexes is influenced by social changes. As an historical reality, this love was closely bound up with religion (the conflicts between the two, a constant theme in the great bourgeois literature, is proof of this), while the family, the structure and social function of which change more rapidly than even sociologists will admit, was the foundation of both.

The person who comes from a well-ordered family, one not forced by destiny out of its proper paths, will retain in adult life something of the child. I would even maintain that maturity has something childlike about it. Without a certain naivete one does not fully grow up. In his earliest movements the child is unaware as yet of any distinction between his surroundings and himself, between the maternal breast and his own body. Only gradually does he learn the variety of objects and names, among them one that is his own; later he learns the further distinction that he speaks only of other people by name and in the third person and speaks only of himself in the first person, as I. The I is the end-result of a long biologico-psychological development in mankind, repeated in shortened form by each individual. If this repetition of the process takes place in an abrupt way and in an overly cold and impersonal atmosphere, then a sense of separateness from others and an unapproachableness remain characteristic of the individual until the end. Love too, in its true form (the kind that embraces everyone, even an enemy), shows traces of the phase prior to the formation of the ego, however extensively that ego may develop. The closer a civilization approaches the point at which the interaction in men of childlike and adult traits is disturbed in the one or the other direction, the more freedom is threatened, for freedom is expanded by the possibilities opened up for identification and love. I believe, therefore, that the Gospel saying, "Become as children," is proving increasingly inadequate in our automatized, regulated world which requires men who will react automatically. With the passing of an economy of individuals competing in relative freedom and the coming of a world of competing states and power-blocs, the religion that appeals to individuals as responsible subjects is losing at least part of its significance to nationalism. The meaning which accrued to every action in life from the thought of eternity is being replaced by an absolutizing of the collective, into which the individual feels himself incorporated.

The more serious and important the subject of discussion, the less important are "You" and "I"; it is the "We" that must come to the fore, even where guilt and innocence are the topic. Here we have the Jewish emphasis on the people, with this difference, however, that at the end there now stands not Messiah but power that lasts for as long as possible. The ultimate goal this power serves is not eternal uprightness or even redemption but the nation. A finite object that swells up in men's awareness into an infinite object necessarily betrays its character as a substitute, even if countless men sacrifice themselves for it more or less freely. Consequently the adherence to such a dubious ultimate meaning for life always tends to become a fanatical mania. European history bears witness, of course, that even a religion in which men do not in their hearts believe and which thus becomes a substitute for itself, can motivate mass slaughter. What distinguishes Peter of Amiens [Peter the Hermit] and Bernard of Clairvaux from the popular demagogues and leaders is their enormous, superhuman betrayal of the very word they preached (although that word was already corrupted and unrecognizable); the totalitarian murders, on the other hand, are innocent of such contradictions. In both cases the disciples make use of what in their hearts they do not believe, in order to avenge on others their own despairing inability to love. This is why the replacement of truth by ideologies, however much the latter may fit the spirit of the times, always brings with it the danger of mass madness. The contemporary efforts of the various religious confessions so to formulate their content as to prevent its degenerating into murderous superstition do not spring simply from the instinct for self-preservation but from objective necessity and the awareness of this danger. There is need, among other things, of overcoming the open opposition of religious people to science, for in the minds of present-day men such opposition does more harm to serious faith than it does to science. The picture of a universe, for example, in which the sun is not simply a speck of dust but is as tiny as an atom (to say nothing of the size of Earth and man) is difficult to reconcile with the idea that God began his creation with the earth and that the redemption of all reality took place here. The phrase, "The One above," which was already out of place in the seventeenth century but which is still used, and not only by pious people (though the latter use it with conviction), is spoken by a child without any idea of its meaning. Initially the phrase referred in a literal way to heaven as "up there"; furthermore, if I am not mistaken, the image of a powerful individual as the highest court of appeal originated in a period when heliocentrism was not yet accepted. The only concrete image today's child can get when he says "The One above" is perhaps that of the industrial manager or the officials in the capital city. That is distressing. People therefore say the phrase is intended symbolically. But the contemporary widespread symbolic interpretation of the religious ideas which can be focused in the term "heaven" is a questionable one. Is God's power really to be understood after the model of political power, though on a more universal scale? If not, why do we find the symbol in question being used not only by children but by their elders as well? For decades now I have discussed this question with Paul Tillich who is, for many contemporary theologians (John Robinson, for example), the source of the symbolic interpretation of important religious categories. What is a symbol whose symbolic meaning no one knows? What is a flag, if it may signify a country or perhaps something entirely different —but a piece of cloth and a pole? If a symbolic content can be the object of thought, then it can be expressed; otherwise a symbol becomes a sign of everything and therefore of nothing.

Symbolic interpretation is an escape route which the despairing take without admitting their despair to themselves. Among the decisive concepts of the Christian religion, if I understand it aright, is that of the individual soul which is inseparably linked with a determinate individual ego. Unlike Buddhism, this doctrine maintains that the soul and the ego are taken into eternity. On the other hand, for contemporary psychology as for the Enlightenment, the ego is the result of an historical and biographical development; it breaks down under the impact of poisons, sickness, and old age, and its perdurance requires unremitting effort. How can we believe that something so fragile and ephemeral as a human ego, however obstinately it may cling to life, is eternal? The paradox must be lessened. Make the eternal soul a symbol and you apparently reduce the opposition between experience and faith. But the concession is dearly paid for. The pain which every lover feels at the transformation of a concept so important for faith into a pure symbol does not disappear in the new outlook. The necessary attempt at symbolization surrenders more than it realizes.

The liberal outlook which inclines to symbolic interpretation as a way of rescuing the idea of eternal truth (an idea which science has long since dispensed with) is opposed by the conservative outlook which clings to the old and traditional in the most literal fashion. To concessions to enlightened views and compromise with rational thought the conservative opposes the piety that repeats verbatim the text of the Bible and traditional ideas. Authority and intolerance must be uncompromisingly defended. Such men, in refusing to be budged, forget that the meaning behind spiritual attitudes can survive only if it can find a new expression which is adequate to changing historical reality. Fidelity to the old is not proved by repeating it but by giving it new expression in word and deed at each historical juncture. If it is to continue to have its original meaning, the traditional must ever anew take a form that is geared to the age and appropriate to it while also contradicting it. Fidelity that does not take the changing world into account is not fidelity at all. Whenever pretensions to power surface in the domestic or external affairs of the Church, whenever the clergy takes on authoritarian traits, the question always arises whether the founder of Christianity, were he to come again, could ever have found a refuge in the Church since its earliest days. In his own day he thought little of prevailing rules and customs; he acted contrary to accepted ways; he was much closer to the heretic than to the orthodox. Would he not have recognized himself in the atheist at the stake rather than in the executioner and judge or in the priest who blessed the whole business? Neither the claim of unchanged validity for the traditional nor its dissolution into symbolism (whatever be the ontological justification offered) can escape the nationalist totalitarian threat abroad today. This if for no other reason than that each of these attitudes displays an intention of continuing to exist in an age that has advanced too far to turn the clock back.

Some manifestations of the regression of freedom in the areas of economy, family, education, politics, and daily life have been pointed out. Among them I regard as decisive the shift of subjectivity from the individual to the collectivity: the clique, the professional caste, the party, the nation. I would include the religious confessions in the list of collectivities to the extent that at times they assert themselves in ways that tend to authoritarianism. The substitution of collectivity for individual even shows itself in the simplest details of daily life. Around 1900 it was up to a person how he crossed the street. He looked right and left, listened for the horse's hooves, and walked, as he chose, slowly or quickly, directly or diagonally, to the other side. Today twenty or thirty pairs of eyes look at the light or the traffic policeman and wait for orders. The signals to which a driver must attend are far more numerous; they determine not only his stopping and going but his tempo and direction. In the larger countries the very form of the curve in the road ahead is reproduced on a sign, and in the ensuing moments the driver must accommodate himself to the little drawing. Pedestrians, like drivers, form a group; both react to directions, and without these directions they could not be thought of as acting at all. In every area of life, even those in which, like the driver, a man reacts as an individual, he thinks of himself as a member, a representative, of a group. The tendency immanent in contemporary society shows in the numbers used for directing the mail. Names of cities are superfluous, an unnecessary extra. It is bad enough to have to remember street names! What is now taken for granted for telephone and automobile will soon be applied to the human individual; the numbers we use for passports, identification cards, and social security are pointing the way. In fact, unless the sign-system is extended to include the individual, the whole administrative process cannot succeed. What happens in society, however, shows its full effects in those who are caught up in the process. Reality forces them to experience their true significance in the social whole. The ideas which can relativize such experience are, in the last analysis, inseparable from theology, and as they fade, the world of numbers is becoming the only valid one; the cultural era in which the individual subject was still unique has come to an end. The awareness of the self as an autonomous individual with his own soul is giving way to the corporate mentality;

I might almost say that the earlier self-awareness is now being unlearned. The phenomenon is not wholly negative in its implications. The movement away from the self-awareness of the ego to the self-awareness of the community, and the negation of the individual which is certainly part of modern life, do have as one element a turning from egoism and from self-love as such. The meaning of the whole process will depend on whether in a regulated world the ego will be raised to a higher level and preserved or simply forgotten.

My remarks here have been inspired by the suspicion of forgetfulness, which is the contrary of fidelity. If my suspicion is justified, then the contemporary development means the radical elimination of the individual, even if that development should lead not to catastrophe but to greater security, the rationalization of society, planning, and the per capita increase of consumer goods for the population. Given the unpredictable nature of individuals it may well be that they will find the elimination desirable. The theory that the individual subject need have no meaning, and the politics based on this theory, are not the exclusive property of Mao Tse-tung, master of the most numerous people on earth and the man whose armies may someday march in our part of the world. The theory and the politics also capture the objective meaning of neo-Positivism, which is the most advanced philosophy is the contemporary Western world. Neo-Positivism is the Enlightenment stood on its head. But here, in accordance with my understanding of the invitation given me, I have spoken only of the problematic freedom of the individual, the freedom without which Christianity is inconceivable.

Notes

FOREWORD

[1] Kant, *Critique of Judgment*, tr. by J. H. Bernard (1892; New York: Hafner, 1951), p. 158.

[2] *Kant's handschriftlicher Nachlass*, in *Kant's gesammelte Schriften* (Akademie Ausgabe), volume 18, p. 130.

[3] Nietzsche, *Nachlass*, in *Werke* (Kröner Ausgabe), volume 15, p. 217.

[4] *Ibid.*

[5] Nietzsche, *Beyond Good and Evil: Prelude to a Philosophy of the Future*, tr. by Walter Kaufmann (New York: Vintage Books [Random House], 1966), p. 104.

[6] This work was reissued in 1969 and translated into English as *Dialectic of Enlightenment* (tr. by John Cummings; New York: Herder and Herder, 1972).

1. THE CONCEPT OF MAN

[1] Kant, *Critique of Pure Reason*, tr. by J. M. D. Meiklejohn (New York: Dutton, 1934), p. 457.

[2] *Ibid.*

[3] *Op. cit.*, pp. 458–59.

[4] *Kant's handschriftlicher Nachlass*, in *Kant's gesammelte Schriften* (Akademie Ausgabe), volume 20, p. 44.

[5] Cf. Eugene N. Anderson, "In Defence of Industrialism," *Diogenes* no. 11 (1955, 3rd quarter).

[6] Gabriel Marcel, *Problematic Man*, tr. by Brian Thompson (New York: Herder and Herder, 1967), p. 139.

[7] Hegel, *Enzyklopädie* I, no. 213.

[8] St. Thomas Aquinas, *Summa theologiae* 11: *Man (I, 75–83)*, tr. by Timothy Suttor (New York: McGraw-Hill, 1970), p. 19.

[9] St. Thomas Aquinas, *Summa theologiae* 13: *Man Made to God's Image (I, 90–102)*, tr. by Edmund Hill, O.P. (New York: McGraw-Hill, 1964), p. 165.

[10] *Nachlass*, vol. 20, p. 8.

[11] Cf. the pertinent works of Arno Schirokauer.

[12] *Nachlass*, volume 20, p. 74.

[13] In *Le Figaro*, September 26, 1956.

[14] Theodor Adorno, "Zum Verhältnis von Soziologie und Psychologie," in Max Horkheimer and Theodor Adorno, *Sociologica: Reden und Vorträge* 1 (Frankfurt: Europäische Verlagsanstalt, 1955), p. 21.

[15] Cf. Reinhold Lindemann, "Gibt es noch europäische Eliten?," *Rheinische Post*, October 20, 1956.

[16] Kant, *Nachlass*, volume 20, p. 159.

[17] Aristotle, *Politics*, Book 7.

[18] Alexis Carrel, *Man, the Unknown* (New York: Harper, 1935), pp. 19–20.

[19] *Op. cit.*, p. 26.

[20] *Op. cit.*, p. 296.

2. THEISM AND ATHEISM

[1] Martin Luther, *Die Hauptschriften*, ed. by H. V. Campenhausen (Berlin, n.d.), p. 409.

[2] Paul H. D. d'Holbach, *Système de la nature*, vol. 3, the Second Year of the Republic, p. 167.

[3] *Ibid.*, vol. 5, p. 211.

[4] Cf. *ibid.*, vol. 1, pp. 23 ff. and pp. 183 ff.

[5] Cf. Pope John XXIII, *Pacem in terris*, Encyclical of April 11, 1963.

[6] Cf. John A. T. Robinson, *Honest to God* (London, 1963), p. 67.

[7] Cf. *Ibid.*, p. 76.

[8] Cf. *ibid.*, p. 114.

3. The Soul

[1] Saint Thomas Aquinas, *On the Truth of the Catholic Faith (Summa contra Gentiles)*, Book 4, chapter 90, tr. by Charles J. O'Neil (Garden City: Doubleday Image Books, 1957), pp. 332-34.

[2] *Op. cit.*, p. 333.

[3] Denis Diderot, *Introduction aux grands principes ou Réception d'un philosophe* (written ca. 1763; published 1798), in *Oeuvres complètes* (Paris, 1875), volume 2/2, p. 84.

[4] Voltaire, *Oeuvres complètes* (Paris, 1882), volume 50, p. 454.

[5] Fritz Mauthner, *Atheismus und seine Geschichte im Abendlande* (Stuttgart-Berlin, 1922), volume 1, pp. 41-42.

[6] Nietzsche, *Werke* (Kröner Ausgabe), Volume 8, p. 167.

[7] In *Frankfurter Rundschau*, volume 14, no. 2 (1967).

4. Schopenhauer Today

[1] Friedrich Nietzsche, *Gesammelte Werke* (Musarion-Ausgabe), München, 1928, vol. XXI, p. 276.

[2] Arthur Schopenhauer, *Sämtliche Werke*, E. Grisebach, ed., Leipzig, n.d., vol. V, par. 57, p. 94.

[3] Schopenhauer, *Handschriftlicher Nachlass*, ibid., vol. III, pp. 32 ff.

[4] *Ibid.*, vol. IV, p. 404.

[5] *Ibid.*, vol. V, par. 126, p. 256.

[6] *Ibid.*, vol. II, p. 520.

[7] *Ibid.*, vol. V, par. 125, p. 253.

[8] Cf. my "Schopenhauer und die Gesellschaft," "Die Aktualitat Schopenhauers," in Horkeimer and Adorno, *Sociologica II*, Frankfurt a. M., 1962, p. 114.

[9] Schopenhauer, *Sämtliche Werke, ibid.*, vol. III, p. 218.

[10] *Ibid.*, p. 216.

[11] Nietzsche, *Gesammelte Werke, ibid.*, vol. VII, pp. 76 ff., quoting Schopenhauer, *Sämtliche Werke, ibid.*, vol. V, par. 172 bis, p. 337.

[12] Hegel, *Sämtliche Werke*, H. Glockner, ed., Stuttgart, 1949, vol. XI, *Vorlesungen über die Philosophie der Geschichte*, pp. 48 ff.

5. THE FUTURE OF MARRIAGE

[1] Num. 12:1.

[2] James George Frazer, *The Golden Bough* 4/1-2: *Adonis, Attis, Osiris: Studies in the History of Oriental Religions* (1914; New York: University Books, 1961; 2 vols. in 1), 4/2, p. 215.

[3] *Op. cit.*, p. 214.

[4] *Op. cit.*, p. 215.

[5] Plato, *The Republic*, tr. by Francis MacDonald Cornford (New York: Oxford University Press, 1941), pp. 159–60.

[6] August Bebel, *Die Frau und der Sozialismus* (Stuttgart, 1901), pp. 427–28.

[7] Voltaire, "Marriage," *Philosophical Dictionary*, selected and translated by H. T. Woolf (New York: Knopf, n.d.), p. 210. [The more recent translation of the whole *Dictionary* by Peter Gay (New York: Basic Books, 1962) does not contain the article on marriage; Gay maintains that this particular essay, along with some others, was not part of the *Dictionary* as Voltaire intended it but was written for Diderot's *Encyclopédie*. —Tr.'s note.]

[8] Nietzsche, *Werke* (Kröner Ausgabe), volume 16, pp. 422–23.

[9] Quoted in Klaus Mehnert, *Soviet Man and His World*, tr. by Maurice Rosenbaum (New York: Praeger, 1961), p. 52.

[10] Cf. Harry Hamm, *China, Empire of the 700 Million*, tr. by Victor Anderson (Garden City: Doubleday, 1966).

[11] Yves de Saint-Agnès, *Révolution sexuelle* (Paris, 1965).

6. THE GERMAN JEWS

[1] Goethe, Letter to Boisserée, June 24, 1816, in *Werke* (Artemis Ausgabe), vol. 21, p. 165.

[2] Jer. 10:2. Some (German) translators, following Luther, speak of "the ways of the heathen." The two versions are in fact not that far apart, since the idol men worship today is the absolutized nation which has lost its roots in the true concept of nation.

[3] Goethe, Letter to Christine Rernhard, May 30, 1807, in *Goethes Gespräche*, in *Werke* (Artemis Ausgabe), vol. 22, p. 456.

[4] Hermann Rauschning, *The Voice of Destruction*.

[5] Helmuth Plessner, *Die vespätete Nation: Uber die politische Verführbarkeit bürgerlichen Geistes* (Stuttgart: Kohlhammer, 1959).

[6] Rauschning, *op. cit.*, pp. 242, 241.

[7] Nietzsche, *Werke* (Kröner Ausgabe), vol. 15, p. 206.

[8] Nietzsche, *op. cit.*, p. 207.

[9] Franz Wedekind, *Gesammelte Werke* (Munich: Georg Müller, 1911ff.), vol. 9, p. 414.

8. FEUDAL LORD, CUSTOMER, AND SPECIALIST

[1] Cf. what is said on pp. 4, 18, 146-147

[2] Cf. pp. 149-151.

9. THREATS TO FREEDOM

[1] Cf. Rene A. Spitz, *The First Year of Life: A Psycholanalytic Study of Normal and Deviant Development of Object Relations* (New York: International Universities Press, 1965).